Inventing the Future:
Information Services for a New Millennium

Contemporary Studies in Information Management, Policy, and Services

(formerly Information Management, Policy, and Services series)

Peter Hernon, series editor

Curriculum Initiative: An Agenda and Strategy for Library Media Programs
   by Michael B. Eisenberg and Robert E. Berkowitz, 1988
Resource Companion to Curriculum Initiative: An Agenda and Strategy for Library Media Programs
   by Michael B. Eisenberg and Robert E. Berkowitz, 1988
Public Access to Government Information, Second Edition
   by Peter Hernon and Charles R. McClure, 1988
Microcomputer Software for Performing Statistical Analysis: A Handbook for Supporting Library Decision Making
   edited by Peter Hernon and John V. Richardson, 1988
The Role and Importance of Managing Information for Competitive Positions in Economic Development
   by Keith Harman, 1989
Statistics for Library Decision Making: A Handbook
   by Peter Hernon, et al., 1989
U.S. Scientific and Technical Information Policies: Views and Perspectives
   by Charles R. McClure and Peter Hernon, 1989
U.S. Government Information Policies: Views and Perspectives
   by Charles R. McClure, Peter Hernon, and Harold C. Relyea, 1989
Library Performance Accountability and Responsiveness: Essays in Honor of Ernest R. DeProspo
   by Charles C. Curran and F. William Summers, 1990
Information Problem-Solving: The Big Six Skills Approach to Library & Information Skills Instruction
   by Michael B. Eisenberg and Robert E. Berkowitz, 1990
A Practical Guide to Managing Information for Competitive Positioning to Economic Development
   by Keith Harman, 1990
Evaluation and Library Decision Making
   by Peter Hernon and Charles R. McClure, 1990

INVENTING THE FUTURE: INFORMATION SERVICES FOR A NEW MILLENNIUM

by

Stan A. Hannah
Nova Southeastern University

and

Michael H. Harris

Ablex Publishing Corporation
Stamford, Connecticut

Library of Congress Cataloguing-in-Publication Data

Hannah, Stan A.
    Inventing the future: information services for a new millenium / by Stan A.
    Hannah.
        p. cm. — (Contemporary studies in information management, policy, and
services)
    Includes bibliographical references and index.
    ISBN 1-56750-450-7 (cloth) — ISBN 1-56750-451-5 (pbk.)
    1. Libraries—special collections—Electronic information resources. 2. Artifi-
cial intelligence—Library applications. 3. Expert systems. I. Harris, Michael H.
II. Title. III. Series.
Z692.C65H35   1999
025.1—dc21   99–26306
                                                     CIP

Ablex Publishing Corporation
100 Prospect Street
P.O. Box 811
Stamford, Connecticut 06904-0811

This one is for Bill, Writha, and Eric

Contents

Preface

In 1998 we published a book entitled *Into the Future,* in which we surveyed and assessed the massive interdisciplinary literature on the "information society" and its implications for library and information services. We were convinced that if library and information scientists were to make true progress in their attempts to understand the present and plan for the future, they required a "social theory of the information society," which would help them make sense of the waves of rhetoric—pro and con—about the future of information services in the United States.

We consider the book, *Inventing the Future: Information Services for a New Millenium* to be a sequel to our earlier work. Here we move beyond the rhetorical contests about the future of the library and turn to the more prosaic but vital task of managing our ever more complex and constantly changing libraries. We conclude that it is of little value to engage in utopian fantasies about the end of libraries, and that what is needed is a blueprint that will guide us in the re-visioning of library and information services. In the pages that follow, we offer one such blueprint—one that will allow us to remain true to our inherited legacy while looking insistently for innovative and effective ways of "inventing" our future.

This book, like its predecessor, is a genuinely collaborative work. We have relied heavily on an extensive body of published literature, and our attempt to confront the interdisciplinary literature on the information era and its implications for library and information services in the United States was greatly aided by the sophistication and comprehensiveness of the published literature. We would also like to thank the hundreds of students who have listened to parts, and finally all, of this book in the form of lectures in two courses taught by the authors. Finally, we owe a considerable debt to our editor, Peter Hernon. He both encouraged us to pursue our desire to understand the role of library and information services in the information era and provided us with very useful guidance in every step of the writing process.

Stan A. Hannah
Michael H. Harris

1

Introduction: The Alexandrian Library Burnt Again

The [19th-century] utopians betray no doubts about their method of selecting books for irrevocable destruction, about the self-evident nature of their morality, or about the permanent character of their own world view. Succeeding ages are denied the right of choosing what they would read for it is assumed that after the introduction of the new order the world view will remain forever the same: thus the new order presumes to have brought historical time to its conclusion. For the modern utopian the destruction of the learning of the past, or its radical revision and reduction, represents the cessation of historical process and constitutes a basic precondition for happiness and justice.
—Jon Theim (1979)

As a consequence of . . . information overload, the role of the libraries for several thousand years, which emphasizes the preservation of the human record, has now become more complex, requiring hard decisions not only about what is to be preserved but also about what is to be discarded. . . . Society needs an agency to digest, evaluate, and make responsible decisions to retain or erase the materials produced.
—Public Library Association

THE USES OF LITERACY: LIBRARIES AND THE MONUMENTAL WEIGHT OF HISTORY

In his brilliant analysis of the symbolic history of the "Great Library of Alexandria Burnt," Jon Theim (1979, p. 507) notes that while modern scholars would agree that the burning of the greatest library of the premodern world represented an "incalculable cultural loss," it must be remembered that "for the *learned* antagonist of letters, the burning of the great library of Alexandria came to be invoked and celebrated." Theim (pp. 522, 523) discusses the extent to which these Nietzschean "suprahistorical thinkers" fantasied that "forgetfulness is the key to equanimity and decisiveness of action." These same men argued that the "integrity of the past is a hindrance to present and future creativity" and thus embraced a "secret longing for a benign state of forgetfulness, a state to efface the malignancy of historical memory." "Such a state of cultural amnesia," Theim suggests, "can be vicariously enjoyed by celebrating the Alexandrian destruction."

Librarians will find an unnerving parallel between the "Enlightenment impulse to order and reduce the immense bulk of the past to the more convenient dimensions of an encyclopedia" and the current gleeful celebration of "the end of the library"— that sad monument to a printed past (Theim, 1979, p. 519). What we appear to be witnessing is a virulent reemergence of the technocratic ideal of the efficient management of "mass society."

For the library technocrats, the only hope for a new, rational, and cost-effective beginning lies in the symbolic burning of the great libraries of the world—an end to library history and the emergence of a new era wherein we will witness the "rapid decline of the *artifact*—particularly the printed book. . .and the replacement of these artifacts with data" (Lancaster, Drasgow, & Marks, 1980, p. 170)—data that will be produced, organized, moved, and explored via information technology (IT). Once again, of course, the impulse is to put an end to triviality, banality, and repetition, to order the modern world of knowledge as if it were a great electronic encyclopedia. In this world view, the "efficient management of information is revealed as the *telos* of modern society" (Winner, 1986, p. 115), and efficiency demands that we accept our destiny as librarians and aggressively carry out our duty to decide what artifacts "to retain or to erase." Such a world view confronts the Alexandrian notion of libraries as great repositories of books reflecting the collective memory of humankind with great hostility. The new technocrats desire nothing less than a second great conflagration—the great library of Alexandria burnt again. It is commonplace to note that F. W. Lancaster's report of the death of the book and its repository, the library, is greatly exaggerated (Harris, Hannah, & Harris, 1998, pp. 18–23). The prospect of millions of books in the Alexandrian libraries of the modern world being metamorphosed into "data" anytime soon is unlikely. However, the hostility among large numbers of librarians to history as represented in millions of printed pages is a subject worthy of sustained reflection (Harris & Hannah, 1992).

The desire to gain control of the "raging book" is a recurring fantasy in the history of the West. Intellectuals and librarians—those most responsible for the production and reproduction of the collective memory—are seized (in a remarkably cyclical way) with a rage for control, for reduction, for simplicity, for relevance. Hidden between the lines in this curious hostility to the book is a fear of the rise of mass society and the decadent tastes of the people (Sosa & Harris, 1991).

Much of the current excitement and debate surrounding the latest round of hostility to the book, encapsulated in F. W. Lancaster's metaphor the "paperless library" (Harris et al, 1998, Ch. 2), was anticipated by the distinguished Spanish philosopher José Ortega y Gasset. In May 1934, Ortega startled librarians and intellectuals everywhere when he delivered an essay entitled "The Mission of the Librarian," wherein he traces the history of the growth of knowledge and the publication of books into his own time. Subtly examining the history of publishing and assessing its implications, Ortega insists that the modern book has become "uncontrollable," and worse: "Many of them are useless and stupid; their existence and their conservation is a dead weight upon humanity which is already bent low under other loads" (quoted in Sosa & Harris, 1991, p. 6).

Complicating the problem is the fact that people tend to read these "useless and stupid" books, stuffing their minds with useless and dangerous "pseudo-ideas." So here you have it: Society is buried in books, many of them useless and stupid, and "the culture which has liberated man from the primitive forest now thrusts him anew into the midst of a forest of books no less inextricable and stifling" (Sosa & Harris, 1991, p. 6).

How should we address this problem? Ortega, unique among the intellectual elite, wonders if it is "too Utopian to imagine in a not too distant future librarians held responsible by society for the regulation of the production of books," with special attention paid to the suppression of "superfluous ones" (Sosa & Harris, 1991, p. 7). Thus, like his postindustrial successors, Ortega recommends that librarians become "masters of the raging book" in the name of efficiency and progress. In a remarkably modern analogy, he insists that his proposals pose no threat to the notion of liberty. All he is suggesting is rational control, or what Daniel Bell (1980, p. 509) might call "the management of organized complexity," prompted by "no more nor less than the need which has demanded the regulation of traffic in the great cities of today" (Sosa & Harris, 1991, p. 9).

When confronting Ortega's insistence that instrumental rationality is the key to the organization of the world of knowledge, most librarians wonder if the cure is not worse than the problem. Many agree with David Berninghausen (1979, p. 13), who declares that the advocates of this new "information paradigm" seem to be suggesting that "librarians claim the responsibility to repudiate the First Amendment by erasing or eliminating what librarians don't like." Such a suggestion, Berninghausen insists, carries intensely antidemocratic overtones and must be categorically rejected by a profession committed to the First Amendment of the U.S. Constitution and the Library Bill of Rights. That is, librarians tend to consider the technocratic suggestion that information professionals should manage information flow just as we would manage traffic flow to be profoundly political. Intellectual-freedom advocates everywhere call for eternal resistance to such a potentially censorial notion. This fear, we think, is well founded, and we wrote an earlier book

(Harris et al., 1998) to inform the debate about such issues as equal access to information, privacy, professional ethics, and corporate responsibility in the age of information.

LIBRARIES, ELECTRONIC LIBRARIES, AND VIRTUAL LIBRARIES

While all schemes to master the book are authoritarian and elitist, they are also inherently irresponsible if they suggest, as does F. W. Lancaster (1978; Harris et al., 1998, Ch. 2), that librarians should simply walk away from the book-filled buildings and set themselves up as information brokers, selling digital information to clients in the private sector.

Surely all responsible professional librarians realize that we can't just abandon the collective fruits of the intellect as represented in untold millions of words on paper so thoughtfully housed and made accessible in the world's great Alexandrian libraries. At the same time, we must be certain that information technologies, electronic writing, and postindustrial communication systems will be effectively deployed by a profession with a 3,000-year history of commitment to the responsible collection, preservation, and effective organization of materials for civilization's racial memory. Our task is to maintain the continuity of humankind's racial memory across this latest of technological divides, to preserve our historic mission to build and manage ever greater libraries of Alexandrian dimensions in these complex and interesting times. To suggest that such a transition will be effortless and without risk is irresponsible and unprofessional.

We have had quite enough of quick fixes and Pollyannish glosses on the information era. We now must turn to the task of managing our Alexandrian libraries into (and through) the postindustrial era. In short, we must not engage in utopian fantasies of the end of library history (Harris & Hannah, 1992) but, rather, get down to the hard work of re-visioning the library in these changing times. We must remain of this world and remain true to its inherited content, but at the same time librarians must look for ways to implement their own future without taking an irresponsible "gamble on the survival of an irreplaceable collection that carries their nation's collective memory" (Higonnet, 1991, p. 33).

BLURRED GENRES: INTERDISCIPLINARY RESEARCH AND THE FUTURE OF LIBRARIES

If we are correct in assuming that change will be neither simple nor immediate, that digital writing will not immediately displace print-on-paper systems, then it follows that we have time to examine our options in re-visioning the library and systematically implement our choices. But what are our options? What choices appear most intelligent? The answers to these questions will emerge slowly as the result of wide-ranging experimentation by thousands of practicing librarians throughout the world. That is, much of the reengineering of the library will emerge from experiential case studies carried out in libraries scattered all across the information environment.

However, this focused experiential reflection and experimentation will need to be critically assessed and selectively deployed as the profession plots its postindustrial future. Moreover, this work must be evaluated within the context of the theoretical and applied work related to the effective deployment of information technology in the global economy. It would be suicidal for librarians to go it alone when millions of information professionals in the corporate and public sectors worldwide are, in many basic ways, similar to those facing librarians. Thus, we flatly reject Ellen Altman's (1979, pp. 293–94) suggestion that librarians "leave history to historians, sociology to sociologists, psychology to psychologists and concentrate our research efforts on topics central to librarianship."

The notion that libraries represent an isolated and unique institution is flawed and dangerous. Rather, our problems are similar to those being addressed by information professionals working in a wide range of institutional and organizational environments. What is clearly needed is a commitment to a collective attempt to identify and apply promising developments from this wider world to problems specific to library and information services. "The skilled problem-solver," Barry Barnes (1982, p. 50) points out, "sees the themes of solved problems in those he seeks to solve." Librarians and information scientists should be able to accelerate change to the extent that they can map and monitor this interdisciplinary research effort and then move analogically from concrete problem solutions in the social sciences to similar, but unsolved, problems in our own smaller world (Harris & Itoga, 1991, p. 348).

Such a commitment will require an intensified effort on the part of practicing librarians, for they will need to break through the walls surrounding the profession in order to probe the adjacent disciplinary landscape. Even then, the task will remain frustratingly complex, for, as Clifford Geertz (1983, pp. 7–8, 24) notes, we are currently adrift in an era of "blurred genres" that is propelling a number of significant realignments in research affinities, resulting in novel interdisciplinary connections "running at some highly eccentric angles." This ferment in the "human sciences" has created a strange and apparently chaotic environment in which all information professionals are in danger of becoming lost. Nevertheless, certain tendencies are emerging; these tendencies, once mapped, promise to afford librarians leverage in their attempt to catch up with the rapidly moving leaders in the race to intelligently deploy the new information technology in the service of their long-standing commitment to knowledge production, storage, organization, and use.

A conscious and systematic attention to interdisciplinary developments offers other benefits as well. One that is especially noteworthy is the possibility that librarians might contribute significantly to the corpus of knowledge emerging about the deployment of information technology. Linking our research to the larger interdisciplinary matrix should allow, even stimulate, librarians to contribute new and confirming analysis to the general effort to manage information resources.

Several other basic considerations must come into play in our collective search for the wisdom that will guide us across the great divide separating print-on-paper systems from the era of electronic writing. One, librarians must recognize the need to critically evaluate their services, both old and new, as we proceed. A lack of attention to evaluation has characterized the profession's activities in the past, but in the future the very cost of doing business will place heavy demands on librarians to produce meaningful and persuasive evidence of the efficacy of the decisions they will be making relative to reengineering the library.

Second, this critical valuative effort must be connected, as never before, with client-centered concerns. Librarians must focus their attention on the most notable blind spot in library services: the needs of users. In the past, librarians have been classic "supply siders," who have spent (quite understandably) a huge amount of time on the identification, collection, preservation, and organization for use of ever larger bodies of printed materials. However, given our obsession with materials, we have lost sight of the real or imagined uses and users of this material. Information services in the postindustrial era must be client-centered, and librarians must develop a new sensitivity to the variety of needs (some old but some quite new) of real information-seekers in the information era.

Finally, any effort to re-vision the library for the 21st century must proceed with a clear sense of the central role that the new technologies will play in the delivery of information services. We cannot imagine a way that librarians can remain central to the information environment without a fundamental commitment to the creation and deployment of a wide range of technologies to contribute significantly in the construction of an effective information-delivery system in the postindustrial era.

New information technologies make possible the creation of integrated digital information systems that will transform the way in which knowledge/information is produced, transmitted, and utilized, both in libraries and in society at large. This transformation will provoke a dramatic re-visioning of the very nature of information services and a radical restructuring of the organizational culture of those institutional sites we now call libraries.

Our insistence that librarians move responsibly into the postindustrial information era should not be read as a Luddite-like call for mindless resistance to information technology and electronic writing. Earlier in this chapter we call for a responsible and thoughtful transition, but readers should not believe that we are advocating a complacent approach to business as usual; even the most casual observer of contemporary library affairs will notice the extent to which new information technologies are restructuring even the largest of our Alexandrian libraries. For instance, in 1994 the Library of Congress announced that it had raised some $13 million from private sources to further its goal of developing a "national digital library" in the U.S. capital. While all informed observers recognize that even this substantial sum will represent only a beginning in the world's largest library, it nevertheless represents a major commitment to the deployment of information technology in the construction of an integrated digital information system.

In the private sector, the signs of the digital revolution are even more apparent. Jeffrey Papows (1998) notes that information technology accounts for an estimated 42 percent of the investment-capital base in the United States.

It is startling figures like this, and hundreds of others from the world of libraries and the private sector, that lead us to believe that the new information technologies promise to provoke a rapid restructuring of the United States' information infrastructure and a steady but dramatic re-visioning of the mission of the nation's libraries in this new context.

These, then, are the essential biases of the work before you. We don't view our focus as particularly controversial, but as you proceed through this book, we hope to provide detailed and persuasive arguments in support of our understanding of the reengineered library of the 21st century—all of this, of course, accompanied by systematic treatment of how that vision might be made real.

2

Paradise Lost or Paradigm Found?

Fate proceeds inexorably only upon the passive individual, the passive people.
—Pearl S. Buck, Address to Nobel Prize winners. New York, December 10, 1942

I hold that man in the right who is most closely in league with the future.
—Ibsen, *An Enemy of the People*

A competitive world has two possibilities for you. You can lose. Or, if you want to win, you can change.
—Lester C. Thurow, *60 Minutes,* February 7, 1988

THE ERA OF DISCONTINUOUS CHANGE

If we had to choose the one characteristic that typifies the essential nature of our age, that characteristic would be change. Even change itself, according to Charles Handy, "is not what it used to be" (1989, p. 4). Handy's observation on the changing nature of change is echoed by Burrus and Gittines (1993, p. 6), who claim that "the emergence of new technology is driving change so fast that change itself has changed." Today change is the norm, and unpredictability is now an inescapable reality that all organizations, including libraries, must confront (Keen, 1991, p. 96).

Although we live in a world dominated by change, we act on the basis of continuity. In *Mastering Change*, Leon Martel notes (1986, p.1):

9

Change is unfamiliar; it disturbs us. We ignore it, we avoid it; often we try to resist it. Continuity, on the other hand, is familiar; it provides safety and security. Thus, when we plan for the future, we prefer to assume present conditions will continue. But they rarely do. As a result, we experience unnecessary losses and miss unseen opportunities. If we could learn to anticipate change and to prepare for it, we could make change work for us, not against us.

Because change now plays such a central role in all institutions, "the best way to prepare for the future is to understand change" (Martel, 1986, p. 1). The first step to understanding change is "to recognize that change is natural and to be expected, and that continuity is unnatural and to be suspected. Because of change, a great deal of what is happening today will be different tomorrow. But though different, much can be known, for change is not random . . ." (p. 1). There are distinct types of change, each with its own pattern, direction, and magnitude. In the next section, we look at discontinuous changes, S-curves, core technology, and paradigm changes in the hope of gaining a better understanding of the implications that rapid, incessant change has for libraries.

Until the 20th century, the rate of technological change was so gradual that the effects of a change would span several generations. This leisurely rate of change allowed individuals and social institutions to absorb new developments over several decades, and individuals and companies were able to hide in the "shadows between the oncoming and receding technologies." "Middle-aged workers could count on retiring," Burrus and Gittines point out (1993, p. 82), "before they had to make major adjustments." In the world of gradual, evolutionary change, the past was the best predictor of the future. It was a world in which:

> Most of the time, for most systems in the world, nothing of any significance happens. Indeed, if you look one minute and then look the next, most of the time you see almost exactly the same thing.
>
> For most systems, of any kind, the best prediction you can make for their behavior in the next instant will be that they will be doing just what they were doing the previous instant. (Weinberg & Weinberg, 1979, p. 3)

Although there are many factors that have contributed to the acceleration in the rate of technological change, most analysts would argue that the preeminent cause is the knowledge economy, which, by creating new knowledge at an explosive rate, has accelerated the process of change. Crawford summarizes this phenomenon in the following words (1991, p. 46):

> Because much new technology is involved in creating and spreading knowledge, the whole process is accelerating as technological innovation creates further innovation. Computers are now designing better computers. Self-generating technological change is at the heart of accelerated knowledge creation, technological change, and the resulting economic, social, and political change.

The increasing rate of change already poses a serious problem for managers. Some management writers have even voiced a "concern about how rapid a rate of change the users can endure, including both top management and middle management" (Madnick, 1991, p. 44). Most "managers see change coming at them at a pace far faster than they can handle" (Keen, 1991, p. 212). The complex nature of technological change makes it particularly difficult for managers, because new technology, by its very nature, is novel and poorly understood. The result, according to Morris and Brandon, is that "business technology is evolving so rapidly that one technology is replaced by another long before many businesses have learned about the first one. To compensate, a business is forced to control new technology by using technical specialists who do not always understand business and who do not effectively converse with business people" (1993, p. 37).

The complications caused by the speed of technological change is exacerbated by the increasingly discontinuous nature of technological change. "A change is discontinuous," according to Ansoff, "whenever it does not directly follow the historical logic of the firm's development" (1988, p. 92). A discontinuous change can be recognized by the extent to which it; alters the way customers are served; reshapes the technology on which the organization's products are based; or modifies the cultural, political, and social settings of the organization (p. 92).

In practical terms, a discontinuous change invalidates the rules and assumptions that determine an organization's operating procedures. Discontinuous change, as Limerick and Cunnington note, "is not just another degree of change—it is a different kind of change" (1993, p. 51). The importance of this distinction can be seen more clearly if we note that in a world of gradual, incremental change, it is sensible to imitate traditional practices and behavior because we expect tomorrow to look exactly like today. When today is the best predictor of tomorrow, the past is a safe and accurate guide to the future. But under conditions of discontinuous change, traditional certainties are thrown into question; our most urgent need is to discover new ways and new rules to operate our organizations successfully (Handy, 1989, pp. 9–10).

COPING WITH DISCONTINUOUS CHANGE

> Unprecedented social, political, and technological changes have occurred during this century. More profound changes lie ahead. To make the decisions that will be required, we must understand the nature of change itself—its causes and effects— its dangers and possibilities. How to create a more desirable and humane future is of urgent and vital concern.
> —Cooper-Hewitt Museum, the Smithsonian Institution's National Museum of Design, *Phenomenon of Change*

The increasing frequency of technological discontinuities remains a critical problem that must be faced by both profit and nonprofit institutions. Foster contends that it is difficult to find an industry in which massive technological change is not looming on the horizon; moreover, the ramifications of technological discontinuities are "enormous, creating an almost unending chain of commercial events that spell success for some and losses for others" (1986, p. 48). Judging by the changes that the Fortune 500 list has undergone in recent decades, Foster is not exaggerating the dangers that technological changes pose for organizations. Less than 35 percent of the original members (since 1955) of this exclusive club remain in business. And the rate of extinction seems to be increasing: A startling 40 percent of the 1970 list had disappeared by 1985. The dangers of institutional inertia and complacency are starkly summarized by Davis and Davidson, who warn (1991, p. 15) that

> the essentials of every business are being altered so fundamentally that you had better not be in the same business five to ten years from now that you are in today.
>
> If after that short time you are still in the same business, it is likely that you will also be on your way out of business altogether.

Many of the most successful organizations have not only recognized the dangers inherent in maintaining the status quo but have modified their organizational culture and rules to explicitly encourage new developments. Perhaps the most famous example is Sony's "sunset" date. "Whenever Sony introduces a new product, for example, it simultaneously sets a 'sunset' date on which it will deliberately abandon that product. This immediately triggers work on developing replacement offerings" (McGill & Slocum, 1993, p. 77). The very successful 3M corporation does not set a sunset date for any of its products. Instead, it avoids product obsolescence by requiring each of its divisions to generate at least 25 percent of its revenue from products that have been introduced within the last five years (Burrus & Gittines, 1993, p. 212).

Product development and life cycles have continued to shrink during the last decade. For instance, in 1990 automobile manufacturers took six years to go from concept to production. In 1996 the cycle time had shrunk to only two years (Tapscott, 1996, p. 63). The change has been even more dramatic in the electronics and computer industries. Hewlett-Packard's head of Computer Systems Organization, Wim Roelandts, states that most of HP's revenues come from products that did not exist a year ago (p. 63). Tapscott (p. 63) claims that "consumer electronics products now have a lifespan of two months." By contrast, some 40 years ago, inventions such as the Polaroid camera and Xerox's copying process guaranteed a revenue that would last a decade or more.

The Importance of Core Technologies

Since "the core technologies of every economy are the ones that provide the foundation on which the rest of the economy is built," the ramifications of changes in core technologies can be enormous (Foster, 1986, p. 48). In today's economy, information technology has replaced the internal-combustion engine and electricity as the core technology (Davis & Davidson, 1991, p. 24). Because the core technology is the basis for revitalization and growth, any changes in information technology will transform the organization so radically that the very nature of businesses—and, accordingly, the way they are managed and organized—is fundamentally changed (p. 51).

For the jaded, the claim that information technology has touched every industry sounds like another example of the customary high-tech hyperbole, which is long on promise and short on performance. Such skepticism, however, is not justified this time; information technology is clearly revolutionizing every product, service, and industry. One of our favorite examples proves that even the humble bathroom is not immune to radical changes. In Japan, automatic, paperless toilets, which give a whole new meaning to the term "paperless society," are now a high-growth item; in the United States, American Standard has introduced a "smart" bathtub that allows the bather to select the temperature, humidity, music, air, and water flow. This high-tech tub also comes with a built-in communications link that allows the owner to program the tub from a remote location (Davis & Davidson, 1991, p. 16). Although these two examples may appear frivolous, they illustrate how information technology can revitalize mature technologies and transform even low-technology products into new ones.

The importance of core technologies can be better understood if we look at what Davis and Davidson call "the architecture of information." Using their classification scheme, information can be categorized in terms of its form and function. *Form* refers to the four basic types of information in widespread use today: data, text, sound, and image. *Function* describes the four things that we can do with information: generate it, store it, process it, and transmit it.

The first function, generation, captures information by converting the information into its digital (machine-readable) equivalent. Once the data has been digitized, it can be loaded into a computer or transmitted over a network. Storing is the second function. Storage simply means that the information is stored in one or more of the four forms, usually on a disk, CD-ROM, or tape. The third function, processing, refers to any type of manipulation of the information, such as editing, synthesizing, or analyzing. Transmission, the last function, is the information age's distribution channel.

Much of the impact that information technology has had on organizations and work can be traced back to some combination of these four functions. For example, a word processor not only stores our manuscripts, but it also allows us to retrieve, copy, and edit them as many times as we wish. It is these qualities—ease of modification, effortless duplication, and rapid transmission—that make a manuscript stored on a disk so much more valuable and flexible than a paper copy of the manuscript.

Core, Defining, and Critical Technologies

Here, we need to address several vital technical questions. First, we privilege the notion of "core technology" in our discussion of information technology because it has become the dominant metaphor in the business and management literature, which we are relying very heavily upon in the construction of our argument. We like the metaphor also because it highlights the extent to which libraries, in their structural and functional characteristics, have been largely framed by their interdependence with core technologies in communication. That is, if the print-based communication technologies were the core technologies of libraries through the last 1,000 years of history, it is obvious that the emergence of integrated digital information systems heralds the arrival of a new core technology in libraries. It is important to note, however, that we might have labeled IT in a different way. David Bolter, for instance, makes a strong case for the fact that we should label IT as the "defining technology" of our era, and he notes that a "defining technology resembles a magnifying glass, which collects and focuses seemingly disparate ideas in a culture into one bright, piercing ray" (1984, p. 11). Or we might have followed Lewis Branscomb (1993), who insists that IT represents a "critical technology" that will tend to dominate other technology in the area of government priorities for technology R&D. But it is important to note that while there is some disagreement over how we should label IT, there is a very wide consensus about its pivotal and hegemonic position in the technology environment.

Another vital issue that must be dealt with here is the matter of "technological determinism." Our emphasis on IT as a core technology should not be construed as a simpleminded endorsement of the notion of technological determinism. We do not endorse the ideology that suggests that technology is autonomous and beyond human control. We have argued at length (Harris, Hannah, & Harris, 1998, pp. 8–11) that technology is a "social construction," and we agree with Jennifer Slack, who insists that technologies are both causes and effects and that IT must be seen as "a part of a complex social formation, and we must explore the particular historically specific effective relationships between those technologies and the social formation in order to critically evaluate those relationships and propose strategies for intervention" (1984, p. 146). We remain adamant, however, in our belief that IT has become the core technology of libraries and that the tough job ahead of us is to decide what to do with it now that we have found it. For excellent recent critical analyses of technological determinism, see Branscomb (1993); Conley (1993); Feenberg (1991); Smith and Marx (1994); and the classic analysis in Winner (1986). For a widely praised analysis of the role of technology in the construction of the contemporary information economy, see Beniger (1986).

Finally, one additional technical point: We are not positing a simple displacement theory of communication technologies. This is why we find the notion of the "paperless library" of little value (Lancaster, 1978). It is apparent that paper-based systems (books and periodicals) will coexist with the ascendant integrated digital systems for the foreseeable future. We have discussed the reasons for this belief at length in Harris et al. (1998, pp. 18–23). We also recommend the work of Petroski (1990) as a useful antidote to all reductionist displacement theories that suggest that the "book is dead" and we are entering a totally digital communications environment. However, having said that, we reiterate our conviction that IT represents the "core," "defining," or "critical" technology of our era and as such promises to slowly but steadily restructure our environment and render paper-based technologies more and more marginal. It follows, of course, that the advent of a new core technology in libraries will provoke a wide-ranging redefinition of the structural and functional characteristics of library and information services in the next century.

Another related economic "benefit is the effective reduction of the cost of reproducing and distributing information—it is often cheaper to duplicate and transmit information electronically rather than in paper or other physical media" (NRENAISSANCE Committee, 1994, p. 113). The ability to access text electronically can present real savings. For example, physicists have enthusiastically developed and used electronic archives in areas such as high-energy physics that are stored at Los Alamos National Laboratory facilities as an alternative to buying journals whose subscriptions cost hundreds to thousands of dollars per year (p. 114). Finally, when information is digitized, its value is enhanced because we can use software to search for keywords, prepare indexes, or perform word-frequency calculations at a fraction of the cost that such processing would cost if we were working from paper copies.

The inherent functional superiority of digital information compared to paper-based documents illustrates how even seemingly minor changes in information technology—today's core technology—can precipitate radical changes in every type of organization from kindergarten to academic library to Fortune 500 company. Of course, IT, which paces organizational change, is itself driven by rapid technological change (Keen, 1991, pp. 227–228). Optical storage, optical character recognition, multimedia, multiprocessor personal computers (PCs), client/server architectures, hypermedia, and expert systems are simply a few of the more prominent innovations that are expected to revolutionize how we use IT in the coming decade.

When changes occur in the core technology so frequently and in so many key areas, we need a new way of thinking about change that will help us to see the implications that underlie individual technological discontinuities. In particular, we want a tool that will help us understand what impact specific technological innovations will have on library services and operations. The product life cycle, an outgrowth of the work of Everett M. Rogers and Theodore Levitt, remains one of the most widely used marketing tools in existence (Rogers, 1983; also see Levitt, 1986, pp. 173–199). The product life cycle typically identifies four stages in the life cycle (Grant, 1991, p. 202):

1. Introduction;
2. Growth;
3. Maturity; and
4. Decline.

The original product life cycle plotted total revenues for a product over time. Richard N. Foster (1986, pp. 31–32) modified the product life cycle so that he could chart the stages that an individual technological innovation undergoes. Although technological innovation is an individual event, Foster observes that innovations go through the same stages of infancy, explosive growth, maturation, and decline (p. 31). When a graph is prepared by plotting the relationship between the effort put into improving a product or process and the returns that one gets *back* on the investment over time, the result is an S-shape curve (p. 22). The S-curve provides a graphic reminder that the pace of technological progress follows a pattern in which a new technology advances slowly at first, then accelerates rapidly, and finally declines (Figure 2.1).

Most people do not find the pattern of development summarized by the S-curve to be surprising. It makes sense that initial progress on developing a new product or process will be slow and uncertain. After all, this is the period when the researchers are struggling to develop the key knowledge necessary to make the innovation practical. Once the fundamental technological problems have been solved, however, the technology takes off. During this stage there may be significant progress for little expenditure of effort. Major improvements take place at a spectacular rate in this period. In time the limits of the technology are approached, and then it becomes more difficult and more expensive to make new advances.

Foster's brief history of the development of rayon provides an excellent example of the S-curve in action. More than $100 million was invested in rayon research

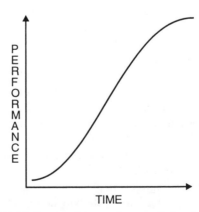

FIGURE 2.1.   S-curve for new technology

and development. However, the investment produced widely varying improvement in performance. Writes Foster (1986, p. 123):

> The first $60 million brought an 800 percent gain over where it began, the next $15 million a 25 percent improvement, and in the early sixties the final $25 million brought only a 5 percent improvement as rayon technology reached its limits.

Although S-curves do not provide an unfailing guide to the future, they do provide a valuable heuristic that can help us answer questions such as, How much change is possible? When can we expect the change to take place? And how much will it cost to make the next round of improvements? Of course, the answers to these questions depend upon our interpretation of our position on the S-curve, which means that the validity of any analysis based on S-curve diagrams ultimately rests upon our judgment about where we are positioned on the S-curve. In addition, "we cannot predict the duration of individual stages or the total life cycle with any accuracy" (Lele, 1992, p. 105). The process is further complicated by innovations that reposition us to a new point on the S-curve. For example, the transfer of data within a computer can never exceed the speed of light (Gazis, 1991, p. 46). Given this fundamental technological limitation, there is a speed limit on the number of operations a computer can perform in a second. However, if we manage to build a computer with multiple processing units and write programs that allow each of the processing units to carry out operations simultaneously, the speed-of-light limitation can be circumvented. In effect, the development of parallel processing computers has created a new technology that repositions computer-processor design from the mature region to the explosive-growth region of the S-curve.

IMPLICATIONS OF THE S-CURVE FOR LIBRARIES

> Current services and products age quickly.
> —James A. Belasco (1991)

The S-curve has many implications for all managers, including library professionals. The most important of these implications include (Foster, 1986) the:

- Dangers of incremental change;
- Marginal return on investment in research on mature technology; and
- Importance of product life cycles.

Until recently organizations had a generation or two to adapt to changing technologies; one set of operating rules might last several lifetimes. But in the current era, librarians face an environment in which "what was right six months ago could become wrong because of a major, rapid change in the environment" (Barker, 1992, p. 155).

When a mature technology, such as vacuum tubes, is challenged by a new technology (transistors) just entering the region of explosive growth, the results can "lead to the demise not only of individual product lines but of whole industries" (Foster, 1986, p. 132). The attempts of the makers of vacuum tubes to protect their markets from change simply increased the costs of failure. The incremental improvements made in vacuum-tube technology were swiftly outpaced by the enormous advances made in the design and fabrication of transistors and integrated chip technology. This example drives home the point that making incremental improvements to a mature technology is very dangerous behavior. The old assumption that innovation is risky has been replaced by a new organizational rule: Innovation is risky, but not innovating is even riskier (p. 30).

Recent attempts to modify the MARC record painfully highlight the futility and high cost of making incremental improvements to a mature technology. The "MARC record" is a complex example of file-based data-processing technology that dominated computer applications during the 1960s. Although cataloguers have attempted to improve subject access for OPACs, the results have been largely disappointing (Adams, 1988, p. 33). This failure can, in part, be attributed to the inherent limitations of the MARC record. For example, it is not possible to revise the MARC record to support hypertext searching or to include support for multimedia formats. The changes needed to support the retrieval of sound, digital music, or bit-mapped images would be so drastic that it would be cheaper and quicker to scrap the MARC record and adopt a totally new format.

S-curves also clarify why investing in mature technologies is subject to diminishing returns. A "mature technology" is one that has been in existence long enough to allow the obvious and high-yield modifications to be made. The technology has been pushed close to its limits; that is, there are not many ways left to improve the performance of the technology. Printing technology is an example of a mature technology that is of great importance to the library community. With minor exceptions, the limits of printing on paper as a technology for conveying information have nearly been reached. In effect, printing is at the upper end of the S-curve; as a consequence, we can expect that any additional refinements will be expensive and will result in only modest improvements (Foster, 1986, p. 34). S-curve analysis suggests that we can expect to see dramatic improvement in both the cost and performance characteristics of electronic documents; on the other hand, there is little likelihood that printing technology will experience any major breakthroughs in cost or performance.

Administrators can learn the importance of the product life cycle from the S-curve. Products and services are created, grow, mature, and eventually decline. If all products eventually become obsolete, as predicted by the product life cycle, then libraries, like every other organization, must constantly develop new products and services to meet changing customer needs. This means that libraries must not only learn how to develop new products and services, but they must also learn how to develop them more quickly. In many industries the ability to develop new products more quickly than the competition has now become a competitive weapon. For instance, in the automobile industry, Honda and Toyota gained a major competitive edge over their rivals by reducing the time it takes to design a new model from five years to three years (Boyett & Conn, 1991, p. 14). It is also important to reiterate that the life expectancy of both products and services is becoming shorter. A generation ago it was not unusual for a product to last for several decades. Today, however, product life cycles have shrunk dramatically (Mitroff & Linstone, 1993, p. 11).

PARADIGM SHIFTS: A TOOL FOR UNDERSTANDING CHANGE

The difficulty lies, not in the new ideas, but in escaping the old ones . . .
—John Maynard Keynes

Since the publication of Thomas Kuhn's *The Structure of Scientific Revolutions* in 1962 (1962/1970), the concept of paradigms and paradigmatic change "has been adopted enthusiastically in fields as diverse as computer science, psychology, sociology, artificial intelligence, linguistics, and information science . . ." (Ellis, 1991, p. 13). This development must have come as a surprise to Kuhn, who originally argued that the behavioral, social, and information sciences were in a preparadigmatic state because they were not guided by a single paradigm. Kuhn subsequently revised his position and conceded that paradigms can also play an important role in multiple paradigm fields—such as the social sciences (1970, p. 179). Ellis concisely summarizes the current status of the role of the paradigm in the following passage (1991, p. 8):

Nor is it the case that only a mature science can be correctly said to have paradigms, or that dual or multiple paradigm science or scientific activity does not exist. On this formulation multiple paradigm fields, such as the behavioural, social and information sciences, are as legitimate fields for the identification of paradigms and analysis of their role, as single or dual paradigm fields such as the physical sciences in their normal and crisis stages.

With or without Kuhn's blessing, the idea of paradigm shifts has been warmly embraced by management analysts as a conceptual tool for understanding the massive changes that have become a commonplace occurrence in today's turbulent environment. By definition, "paradigms are systems of interrelated ideas and techniques that offer a distinctive diagnosis and solution to a set of problems" (Guillen, 1994, p. 7).

A paradigm, thus, is "a mental frame of reference that dominates the way people think and act." It is, continues Karl Albrecht, "a way of connecting ideas, prioritizing values, approaching issues, and ultimately forming habit of behavior with regard to a subject" (1992, p. 45). In short, "paradigms are functional because they help us distinguish data that is [*sic*] important from that which is not" (Barker, 1992, p. 152).

Because paradigms are rules for seeing and observing, they are powerful, two-edged swords. When used correctly, they can cut the world into discrete bits of refined information that give the paradigm practitioner very subtle vision (Barker, 1992, p. 90). When used in the wrong context, the paradigm cuts the practitioner off from data that contradicts the paradigm. As a result, "we see best what we are supposed to see. We see poorly," continues Barker, "or not at all, data that does not fit into our paradigm" (p. 91).

All of us have our paradigms that explain the way things work. Paradigms are created when (Barker, 1992, p. 48) "people tackle a new problem and develop successful patterns for dealing with it. These patterns tend to form around an underlying 'theory' or a frame of reference that makes the approach consistent and communicable."

Over time there is an almost irresistible temptation to convert a successful paradigm into "the paradigm." Inevitably, however, organizational paradigms become "outmoded, obsolete, dysfunctional, or antagonistic to progress when the original problem condition changes and the original paradigm fails to change with it" (Albrecht, 1992, p. 48). Unfortunately, "the need to change a paradigm" becomes evident only when we realize that the old rules no longer work (1992, pp. 47–48).

Because a paradigm shift represents a change to a new game and a new set of rules, one can destroy entire industries. For example, by 1968 Switzerland had dominated the world of watchmaking for 60 years. Not only did the Swiss make the best watches in the world, but they were constantly improving their watches. They had invented the minute and the second hands; they were leaders in research in waterproofing watches and marketing the best self-winding watches. It was no wonder that they had more than 65 percent of the sales of the world watch market and 90 percent of the profits.

By 1980 Switzerland's market share had collapsed to less than 10 percent. The paradigm shift had altered the fundamental rules of watchmaking. As a result, between 1979 and 1981, 50,000 of 62,000 Switch watchmakers lost their jobs. Barker notes (1992, p. 17):

> The irony of this story for the Swiss is that the situation was totally avoidable if only the Swiss watch manufacturers had known how to think about their own future. If only they had known the kind of change they were facing: a paradigm shift.
>
> The Swiss, after all, invented the electronic quartz movement, but Swiss manufacturers rejected the idea in 1967. Since it did not share their view of a watch, it couldn't be the watch of the future. They were so sure that the quartz movement had no future

that they let their researchers showcase their useless invention at a trade fair. Seiko took one look and bought the rights to the watch.

This example also illustrates that "when a paradigm shifts, everyone goes back to zero" (p. 140). All of the Swiss's hard-earned skills at fashioning accurate gears, flawless bearings, and superb mainsprings, which were so important in the old paradigm, were totally worthless when the digital-watch paradigm replaced the mechanical-watch paradigm (p. 144).

Paradoxically, because Switzerland's watch industry was so good at producing mechanical timepieces, the Swiss were particularly vulnerable to the changeover to digital technology. Their long history of success made them reluctant to abandon a technology that they knew better than anyone else in the world. When the successful habits of a lifetime suddenly become obsolete, it is understandable that most people choose to continue business-as-usual. The result, as Richard Crawford observes, is that "the very products, procedures, and organizational forms that helped businesses succeed in the past often prove their undoing" (1991, p. 110).

Given the power of a paradigm to "govern our lives and dominate our thinking processes," it comes as no surprise that outsiders are the most likely catalysts for change (Albrecht, 1992, p. 47). Some famous examples include Dan Bricklin, Almond B. Strowger, and W. Edwards Deming. Although Bricklin invented the electronic spreadsheet, he was not an accountant; in fact, he created the electronic spreadsheet to help him get through his beginning finance course (Levy, 1989, p. 318). His knowledge of accounting was so rudimentary that he had to refer to an introductory textbook while he was writing the code for the program that eventually became famous as *Visicalc*—the program that revolutionized accounting practices. Bricklin's teachers at Harvard, the experts in the old paradigm, "thought he was wasting his time" on a program that no manager would ever want to use (Levy, 1989, p. 319).

W. Edwards Deming, the famous leader of the quality revolution, was a statistician who became famous as a production expert (Barker, 1992, pp. 58–59). But the ultimate outsider has to be Almond B. Strowger. Strowger, an undertaker, revolutionized the Bell telephone system by inventing the automatic switching and rotary dialing system, which made it possible to place calls without operator assistance (pp. 65–66). These examples illustrate that dramatic changes in a field are rarely brought about by experts in the old paradigm. As Barker notes (p. 70):

How often has an important innovation in technology or business, or education, or any field that is doing well, come from the established practitioners? Rarely. Because if you are doing well using the old paradigm, it makes no sense to turn around and put yourself out of business by creating a new set of rules. It makes much more sense for you to continue to improve what you are already good at.

Most important, we must remember that a paradigm is basically a way of looking at the world based on a set of shared assumptions. Our paradigm may be based on very useful and conceptually powerful assumptions; but they are still assumptions, liable to become invalid when the environment changes.

THE REVOLUTIONARY NATURE OF DIGITAL INFORMATION

> Digital information is forever. It doesn't deteriorate and requires little
> in the way of material media.
> —Andrew Grove

As librarians prepare to enter the next millennium, they confront a future that is a disturbing mixture of threat and opportunity, where rapid, unremitting change is the only certainty. While it would be comforting to believe that libraries will remain a uniquely privileged institution, sheltered from the harsh winds of change because their services constitute a public good, there is a growing body of evidence that libraries already confront a paradigm shift. In particular, the importance of information technology as the major means of creating wealth by adding value to services and products has become the central tenet of business strategists. Davis and Davidson, for example, write that "all economic activities will depend upon information to create and control their destiny" and "that the economic value from generating, using, and selling information is growing significantly faster than the value added by producing traditional goods and services" (1991, p. 17). The expanding role of information, as well as our increased ability to store and process this imperishable and continuously accumulating resource, makes information, according to Leon Martel (1986, p. 38), the most important agent of change in the postindustrial society. Martel notes the revolutionary qualities of digital information (1986, pp. 37–38; see also Harris et al., 1998, pp. 3–5):

> Johann Gutenberg's invention of movable type enormously increased distribution of the printed word, making possible widespread literacy; but the means to electronically store and retrieve information is a far greater structural change, comparable only to the invention of writing itself, for it has created a wholly new form of preserving, manipulating, and displaying information, with capabilities which completely dwarf that of the printed page.

The revolutionary nature of digital data can best be illustrated by looking at an embryonic industry still several years away from market success: the electronic book. The Sony Data Discman combines CD-ROM technology with a microprocessor to create the first electronic book. This small unit comes with a Liquid Crystal Backlit screen, which, according to Sony's brochure, can be read in any kind of light. This is a slight exaggeration, since the unit is difficult to read in bright sunlight. However, much to the chagrin of book lovers everywhere, the Discman is one computer that is designed to be read in bed. At present the Discman's modest price (currently about $140) and enormous storage—the equivalent of 80,000 pages of text—make it a natural way for students to have immediate access to a dictionary, a thesaurus, or textbooks.

The Discman turned out to be a flop. It was too heavy, too hard to read, and too fragile (Lemos, 1998). Despite the Discman's poor sales record, however, the industry remains sanguine about the future of the electronic book. Three new entrants into the market, Rocket eBook, Everybook, and Softbook debuted in the last quarter of 1998. With a lower price, a more legible screen, a lighter weight, and new features, the makers of these electronic books are targeting the corporate market.

While the electronic book is admittedly in its infancy, it does illustrate the enormous disruptive power of a paradigm change. For example, what would a switch to electronic books mean for the publishing industry? To understand the implications of a switch from paper to digital books, let us look at the special skills that publishers currently need to publish a book and then contrast their current skills with those that will be needed to publish an electronic book.

To publish a paper-based book, publishers typically need to be able to:

- Buy rights to a book;
- Edit the manuscript;
- Set the type;
- Design the book cover;
- Print a large number of copies at a low cost;
- Market the books;
- Distribute the books; and
- Pay royalties.

The expertise needed to publish an electronic book clearly shows how the rules of the game have changed. While publishers still need to be able to buy rights to a book, edit the manuscript, and market the resulting books, an electronic publisher will not need to set type, print the book, or bind the book (Barker, 1992, p. 146). But the biggest change, and potentially the most profitable change, is that publishers will no longer need a physical distribution system. Instead of printing the books, storing them in warehouses, and then shipping the volumes to bookstores, publishers will be able to transmit entire books over the Internet. Since the electronic books will have the ability to write on an empty disc via a modem, the entire, expensive distribution system of the publishing industry can be replaced by an optical communications link and a modem. The same program that oversees the transmission of the "book" to buyer will also charge for connect time, author royalties, and the fee for the electronic distributor (p. 146). In effect, the change from paper-based to digital media has changed the channel of distribution, thereby making it possible to eliminate book inventories by supporting "just-in-time" book delivery. In addition to eliminating inventory costs, the switch to electronic media will mean no shipping costs, no returns, no out-of-print books, and no delivery delays until the next printing cycle (Silberman, 1999). In the long run, the electronic book offers some real advantages over the codex. In the first place, the price of a book in electronic format should fall to around $3.00 or $4.00 (Lemos, 1998). Even more appealing, improvements in the storage density of electronic books will mean that one electronic book will have the capacity to store 200,000 books, which means that the electronic book will really be more like carrying around one's own personal library than a few books (Lemos, 1998).

Finally, Martel (1986, p. 67) observes that although "books have the longest and strongest future among the print media," eventually they too will be "overtaken by the long-term structural shift to electronic media of communications." Since the price of electronic publications is expected to continue to fall relative to that of traditional print publications—as predicted by S-curve analysis—electronic media will gradually replace the familiar paper-based books and journals whenever cost is a significant consideration. The potential savings may be substantial. According to Christinger Tomer (1993, p. 156), if publishers were to switch to producing electronic journals, their savings on the costs of printing, binding, and shipping would slash operating costs by as much as 75 to 80 percent.

This same point was made more emphatically by the executive director of the Association for the Advancement of Science (*OCLC Newsletter*, 1992, p. 33) when he noted, "The pure economics of today's world will inevitably drive publishers to electronic publishing . . . in my opinion, the economic driver is inexorable."

However, it should be noted that the savings involved in electronic publishing are intensely contested, with some arguing that only about 25 percent of the cost of operating a scholarly journal could be saved by going digital (Bryant, 1994, p. 149; also see Lancaster, 1995). Whatever the amount, everyone agrees that the savings would be substantial and that these savings combined with the speed of digital publication do indeed seem to promise that the transition will proceed at an ever more accelerated pace.

Such a paradigm change will also have an impact on other members of the publishing industry. Obviously, small bookstores might lose a significant part of their sales if a centralized national bookseller offered to sell "digital copies" at a reduced price. No doubt, technological determinists will hurry to announce the inevitable demise of the local bookstore; however, such a simplistic analysis ignores the important role that browsing plays in the decision to buy a book. The important point to note is that changes in the channel of distribution can have a major impact on entire industries and that the members of the publishing industry must rethink their role and the services they provide. In other words, the old rules and assumptions have been invalidated by a paradigm shift.

The publishing industry offers another example that demonstrates the importance of changes in distribution channels. Because of shipping costs, publishing was originally a local business. With the advent of new mass-transportation technologies—railroads and the internal-combustion engine—printing became a national business. Now the switch to an electronic channel of distribution will allow the publishing industry to become "a global business" (Davis & Davidson, 1991, pp. 77–78).

THE REVOLUTIONARY NATURE OF INFORMATION TECHNOLOGY

> In the 1990s, there is no status quo. The velocity of change in
> information technology has seen to that.
> —Don Tapscott (1996)

Information technology, defined by Emery as "the technology associated with the computer hardware, computer software, and communications," is now recognized as "vital to the long-term success of virtually all organizations" (1987, pp. ix, 317). Gibson and Jackson (1987, p. xviii) summarize the accepted view of the importance of information technology in the following statement: "Sooner or later, every industry, every firm, and every career will be surrounded by, dependent upon, and required to respond to information technology and its implications. The only question is how and when."

Although millions of people now use computers on a daily basis, David Vaskevitch, the director of Microsoft's Enterprise Computing Division, argues that *"in spite of this, the computer revolution is only now about to begin"* (1993, p. 1, emphasis added). Vaskevitch continues (p. 2) that

> most organizations still operate quite similarly to the way they did in the '50s, and although computers have simplified and sped up many processes, they have hardly revolutionized the way most businesses run.
>
> In the next ten years, computers will finally change the fundamental way people organize and run businesses of all sizes.

It is tempting to regard Vaskevitch's prediction as just one more example of the exaggerated claims that are such a staple of high-tech prognostications. However, his argument cannot be dismissed so cavalierly. Organizations, in both the public and private sectors, have used information technology "to mechanize old ways of doing business. They leave," Hammer (1990, p. 104) continues, "the existing processes intact and use computers simply to speed them up." The result of automating the old, manual systems is summarized in a 1993 *Business Week* article ("The Technology Payoff," 1993, p. 58):

Throughout the 1980s, U.S. businesses invested a staggering $1 trillion in information technology. For a long time, it looked as though most of that money was going down a rat hole.

And, most troubling of all, in the service sector, where businesses sank more than $800 billion into technology, the results were the worst.

But in the past few years, organizations are "finally making the information revolution pay off" ("The Technology Payoff," 1993, p. 57). There is a growing realization that before we can exploit the full potential of information technology, we must radically redesign our 19th-century organizations to cope with the challenges of the 21st century. In Hammer's words (1990, p. 104):

It is time to stop paving the cow paths. Instead of embedding outdated processes in silicon and software, we should obliterate them and start over. We should "reengineer" our businesses: use the power of modern information technology to radically redesign our business processes in order to achieve dramatic improvements in their performance.

Libraries, like all other information-intensive organizations, must begin to rethink and redesign their processes and operations. The only way to take advantage of the benefits offered by the switch from paper documents to electronic documents, from mainframes to client/servers, from centralized to distributed databases, and from text to multimedia is to reinvent our organizations. It is this organizational revolution that underlies Vaskevitch's prediction that "computers will finally change the fundamental way people organize and run businesses of all sizes" (1993, p. 2). For libraries the first harbingers of the coming electronic revolution are already visible.

THE INTERNET AND THE DIGITAL LIBRARY

Without question, the Internet is the most visible sign of the electronic revolution for librarians. No library journal, conference proceeding, or workshop is complete without at least some reference to the Internet. Originally, the primary Internet application was electronic mail, but "a second generation of applications that are very different from e-mail" is now available (NRENAISSANCE Committee, 1994, p. 61). The second-generation applications provide a means for users "to explore the information space and to retrieve desired information elements. These applications—which include archie Gopher, the World Wide Web (WWW) and its Mosaic interface, and the Wide Area Information Service (WAIS)—are redefining the future of the Internet and providing a whole new vision of networking" (p. 61).

Even in its nascent state, the Internet has assumed many of the functions that were formerly carried out by libraries. Historically, a major function of libraries has been to serve as distribution centers for documents. As early experience with the Internet has shown, electronic databases and full-text digital documents not only serve as central storage facilities (the library function), but they also allow Internet the capability to disseminate a perfect copy of the desired document anywhere, anytime, and in any format. It is this capability that makes practical Vice President Albert Gore's vision of the digital library, which he described as follows (Gore, quoted in *Lexington Herald-Leader*, 1994, p. 24):

> No longer will geographic location, wealth, gender or any other factor limit learning. One of my ideas for the information superhighway is that a child from my hometown of Carthage, Tenn., will be able to come home from school, turn on a computer and plug in to the Library of Congress in Washington, D. C. He or she will be able to find information on any topic from all over the world by browsing through vast digital libraries.

Whether we call them digital, electronic, virtual libraries, or "libraries without walls," the online, networked library differs from the traditional library in several key ways:

- Compact data storage;
- Ease of data manipulation; and
- Accessibility and interactivity.

Since "knowledge has been doubling about every seventeen years since the time of Newton," the ability of digital libraries to store enormous amounts of information is a significant advantage (Denning & Metcalfe, 1997, p. 73).

Because digital information can be stored so compactly, digital libraries do not require large, expensive buildings to house the acres of shelving needed to store print documents. When the Columbia Law School library encountered space problems, the alternatives were either to expand the library, at a cost of around $20 million, or to store the documents in digital format (Cage, 1994, p. A27). After considering the various tradeoffs, the administration and the library decided that substituting optical storage technology for construction costs was a more cost-efficient solution.

The second noteworthy characteristic of digital libraries is that "the use of an electronic digital format means that data of any kind can be potentially communicated, analyzed, manipulated, and copied with ease" (NRENAISSANCE Committee, 1994, p. 138). It is this ability to share documents that secondary teachers have found to be particularly useful. When teaching materials are available on the Internet, they can be quickly duplicated because they are stored in a digital format. As a result, "everything from lesson plans to laboratory exercises to curriculum development guides is now being used by classroom teachers. In most cases they can use the material quickly with a minimum of fuss on their part" (p. 129).

Although "the digital library is not a single entity or database in a specific geographic location," modern communications technology allows researchers or even casual users to interact with individual databases, regardless of their location (p. 138). It is truly a library without walls.

The digital, or virtual library, thus, represents a new paradigm of library service. It is a library that, in theory, offers access to anything, in any digital format, at any time, and at any place. It comes as no surprise that "people are so taken with a virtual library that they just want it yesterday" (Mandel, quoted in Cage, 1994, p. A23). It is also a library that comes directly into the home or office of each customer.

According to the NRENAISSANCE Committee, the evolution of Internet has already changed "the nature and mix of services provided by libraries" (1994, p. 136). In particular, "Internet access enables libraries to leverage their resources so as to acquire more of the scholarly record, and to own materials collectively and share them between libraries and their end users" (p. 136). The ability to access digital documents has, in some cases, led libraries to reduce their spending for print-based monographs and serials. The Los Alamos National Laboratory, for example, has used electronic archives in areas such as high-energy physics "as an alternative to buying journals that cost hundreds to thousands of dollars per year for subscriptions" (p. 114). Perhaps an even more impressive harbinger was the Commonwealth of Virginia's dramatic announcement that it planned to invest $5.2 million in a "statewide virtual library." Of this total, $2 million would be spent exclusively on electronic library materials.

While the vision of the digital library, with its effortless access to a seamless web of interrelated networks, has enormous appeal, converting even one library's collection so that it can be accessed over a local area network (LAN) has proven to be enormously complicated (Conway, 1994, pp. 42–45). Once these technical issues are resolved, the even tougher challenges of developing a system for protecting copyrighted material and ensuring that the digitized documents accurately duplicate the original texts must be faced (Cage, 1994, p. A23). While we agree with Jean Bechtel (1986, p. 220) that being adrift in a "vast sea of information and technological advances" has undermined our "confidence in who we are and what we are to do," we also share her conviction that there is little room for delay in finding a "more powerful alternative to the old rules and visions."

RESEARCH AND THE DIGITAL LIBRARY

Despite the complex problems facing the developers of digital libraries, there is compelling evidence that the changeover from print-based libraries is already under way. In November 1993 the National Agricultural Library (NAL) made the following announcement (Ditzler, Early, & Weston, 1993, p. 2):

The world of information management is changing daily. The current paper-based information delivery system is inadequate to keep pace with the needs of the modern agriculturist. Increasingly, information is produced in digitized form, and with recent telecommunications innovations and the Internet, the resources available to the computer literate researcher are expanding exponentially. The length of time expended for traditional publication, procurement, physical handling, indexing and document delivery processes is no longer acceptable. Transition from the traditional print collection to the "electronic library" will necessitate a shift from a production mode to a facilitator mode of service.

To carry out its role as the national distributor of agricultural information, the NAL has decided that it must now collect, store, and distribute U.S. agricultural information digitally. To demonstrate its commitment to meeting the challenges of becoming an "electronic library," on January 1, 1995, the National Agricultural Library announced that it would designate electronic information the preferred medium (Ditzler et al., 1993, p. 3).

The National Agricultural Library's commitment to electronic documents is far from unique. Researchers in areas as diverse as biomedical research, particle research, the Beowulf project (textual analysis database for manuscripts), and the Perseus project (a multimedia database for the study of ancient Greece) are only a few of the research projects in which the Internet performs many of the functions traditionally carried out by research libraries such as the collection, storage, and distribution of research materials (NRENAISSANCE Committee, 1994, pp. 114, 118).

While it may be premature to argue that "the nature of research is itself changing," there is no doubt the Internet has provided a powerful tool that allows researchers to interact with their colleagues, share data and computational resources, and access bibliographic and whole text information in digital libraries—all without regard for geographical location (pp. 115–116). In effect, information technology has been used to create a virtual laboratory (often referred to as a "collaboratory") where researchers on different continents and from different disciplines can conduct joint experiments.

Researchers in the humanities have also recognized the advantages that electronic documents, available on global networks, have for conducting textual research. Alan T. McKenzie (1994, p. 201) notes that "even those academics who still pride themselves on their technological antipathies" must concede that online textual databases are rapidly becoming a vital resource. After all, "If a humanist is someone who takes texts too seriously, then humanists ought to venture on line, where texts, serious texts, may be sent further and received faster, with less effort and expense, than even Dr. Faustus might have imagined."

Paul Delany (1993, p. 197), however, wistfully concludes, that "there can be no substitute for the aura that print culture has accumulated over the centuries; but the usefulness to scholarship of computerized knowledge management ensures that, in the century that awaits, these technologies are bound to prevail." Once a text has been digitized and text-analysis software has been coded, "literary text analysis can be carried out with unprecedented detail," speed, and sophistication (NRENAIS-SANCE Committee, 1994, p. 118).

For libraries the combination of laboratories without walls accessing a digital library that exists only as a series of databases scattered throughout the world represents a dramatic change in the library's role as a channel of distribution. Historically, libraries have served researchers by collecting, housing, and disseminating information stored on paper. The traditional goal of every research library has been to amass as large a collection as possible in the hopes that the sheer magnitude of the collection would make it possible for the library to own every document that a researcher might request. The test of a quality library was, in the words of the library profession's prototypical scholar-librarian, "its ability to get into the hands of the reader the book he wants when he wants it." And since it was axiomatic that "the odds of success are obviously better if we have more books," the mission of the librarian was quite simple: "Raise all the money we can to acquire and house all the books we can" (Harris & Tourgee, 1983, p. 57).

This "just-in-case model" of collection development made sense in a world in which information could be shared only by the time-consuming process of sending either the requested book or a physical copy of the desired article. In a world of digital documents, however, the ability to transmit electronic copies now makes resource sharing so quick and inexpensive that it allows research libraries to move away "from the 'just-in-case' model of on-site resources to the 'just-in-time' model of resource sharing" (NRENAISSANCE Committee, 1994, p. 136).

The ability to disseminate information as a digital message rather than as a physical artifact promises to have an equally great impact on the future role of the public library. Brewster Kahle, one of the principal architects of the Wide-Area Information Server (WAIS), predicted that when electronic document transmission becomes commonplace (1991),

> access and archiving become quite different, since making a copy is easy and inexpensive, and delivering a copy can be done without requiring a person to come into the library. . . . The result of this technology change can be an existing one where the public library system can refine its charter and serve the public in a . . . way that was not possible with paper. The unique aspects of libraries—service oriented staff, lack of profit motive, prevalent locations, and the role in schools—can give them a more important role.

We are left with Richard Lanham's (1993, p. 134) haunting refrain: "The library world feels *depayse* today . . . both of its physical entities, the buildings and the books they contain, can no longer form the basis for planning."

Professor Lanham draws the now all-too-apparent conclusion that our "curatorial function has metamorphsed" and that librarians must turn to the task of "consciously" building "human attention structures" and abandon the outmoded ritual of assembling massive book collections "according to some commonly accepted rules."

3

Crossing the Postindustrial Divide

PROBLEMS, OLD, NEW, AND ELECTRONIC

Access is more important than ownership in the new online environment.
—Thomas Peters (1991)

Remote Access

Of all the changes made possible by information technology, probably none is potentially more revolutionary than the ability to access library materials from remote locations. It is difficult not to agree with Thomas Peters' claim that "remote access will affect the structure, usage, economies, and politics" of the library (1991, p. 3). Thirty years ago "a library's stock-in-trade consisted of books, journals, newspapers, and manuscript materials, and the only means of access was the library's card catalog" (De Gennaro, 1987, p. 7). In that era the size and quality of the collection were the most important measures of the value of the library.

De Gennaro explains why the size of the collection was so critical for library clients (p. 7):

> Those who wanted access to library materials had to come to the library and either use them in the building or borrow them for home use. If a library did not have what the patron wanted, he either had to send for it on interlibrary loan, which took up to three months, or he had to find out where it was and go to that library.

There was a strong correlation between collection size and accessibility. Users knew that "if the library owned the item, chances were good that the patron could gain easy access to the item" (Peters, 1991, p. 26). This strong relationship between the size of the central collection and client satisfaction led to the common practice of evaluating a library by the size of its collection. Historically, the great libraries were considered great because they had the largest collections. The Alexandrian Library, the Library of Congress, the British Museum—to list but a few of the most famous libraries—were prized in large part because of the sheer size of their collections. By the middle of the twentieth century, collection size was so strongly equated with the quality of the library that academic and research libraries frequently competed with one another by comparing the number of volumes that they owned.

Remote access breaks the relationship between ownership and accessibility. And since "users always have been interested more in easy access to information than in questions of ownership," the digital library promises to redefine what is meant by "great library" (Peters, 1991, p. 26). In the world of the digital library, the "greatness" of a library is more likely to be defined by its ability to access information and provide value-added services than by the size of its collection (Woodsworth et al., 1989, p. 134).

Since remote access breaks the relationship between accessibility and ownership, electronic libraries will no longer need to own and warehouse the materials to which they provide access. This represents a major shift in the library's historic role as the storehouse of the book. In Seiler and Surprenant's conception of the electronic library of the future, the library becomes "the most massive database yet created." Moreover, "there will be no books, journals, shelves, or reading tables inside these electronic libraries. No users will need to visit them. All access will be accomplished from remote locations via the network" (Seiler & Surprenant, 1991, p. 30).

In a similar vein, Peters wonders if libraries might someday "become communication networks and file servers" that exist only as a telephone number or address on the Internet (1991, p. 237). At this point in time, it remains unclear what the long-term implications of remote access have for libraries and the library professional. What is clear, however, is that remote access represents a paradigm shift that profoundly challenges many of the basic assumptions we have about the role of libraries. And while it is apparent to all that our responsibility for the paper-based collective memory of our society will continue to be central to our mission, it also seems obvious that contemporary knowledge production is going digital.

Bibliographic Control in the Digital Library

The remote access of digital information has also created a whole new set of problems that either invalidates or makes irrelevant many of the established rules of bibliographic control. The magnitude and nature of the problem of providing access to distributed digital information can best be understood by looking first at the Internet's current access tools and then at the traditional bibliographic control tools used by librarians.

The most striking feature of the Internet is the growth rate of this network of networks. By 1994 a new computer was being added to the Internet every 30 seconds (Comer, 1995, p. 70). During the decade from 1983 through 1994, the number of computers on the Internet nearly doubled every year (p. 70).

The actual number of users remains a matter of guesswork. The Internet Society estimates that there are between 20 million and 30 million active Internet users (Ayre, 1994, p. 120).

While the number of Internet users can be only roughly estimated, the total number of files and documents available on the Internet is not just unknown, but it also changes with every passing nanosecond. Since the hallmark of the Internet is constant change, providing access to its millions (or is it billions?) of documents constitutes an enormous challenge. Early efforts to provide searching tools for the Internet concentrated on locating files. *Archie* (short for archive) makes it possible to locate files stored on file transfer protocol servers by building a global index for all the anonymous file transfer protocol sites on the Internet (Ayre, 1994, p. 128). In other, and hopefully clearer, words, archie allows us to search for specific file names; in this respect, archie corresponds roughly to a title search in a library.

Gopher, developed at the University of Minnesota, was an attempt to make it easier to list and retrieve files by allowing users to browse the Internet using an interactive menu (Comer, 1995, pp. 190–191). Gopher simplifies the task of searching for electronic documents by "reducing nearly everything to menus" (Levine & Baroudi, 1993, p. 229). Instead of searching for a specific file name, we can now search for information by working through a series of interlocking menus that organize the information by topic, such as phone books, computer information, fun and games, and libraries.

It almost sounds as if Gopher menus provides reliable subject access. Unfortunately, they do not. Because Gopher is a totally decentralized system, there is not a "great deal of consistency from one menu to another"; in fact, "anyone who wants to can put up a Gopher server" (Levine & Baroudi, 1993, p. 234). The good news is that volunteers have created hundreds of Gopher servers on the Internet; the bad news (p. 234) is that

> almost none of these people have any experience in indexing and information retrieval (for that you'd need a degree in library science), so the same item may appear on five different menus under five different names, and no two Gopher menus are quite the same.

The World Wide Web provides a menu with hypertext links that are used to access related multimedia documents (Comer, 1995, pp. 209–211). The hypertext links are created by inserting them into documents using hypertext markup language (Ayre, 1994, p. 132).

Another major searching tool available on the Internet is the Wide-Area Information Server. WAIS provides full-text indexing software that is used to index large text files, documents, and periodicals (Ayre, 1994, p. 134). WAIS allows Internet users to "locate a set of documents that contains a given term or phrase" (Comer, 1995, p. 240). WAIS is one of the most powerful automated search services available on the Internet. Like conventional document retrieval systems, WAIS permits searchers to identify sample documents and use them to find additional documents that are similar (Comer, 1995, p. 240).

From even this brief description of the Internet's searching and browsing tools, it is obvious that authority control and controlled vocabulary play no role in searching the Internet. There is no online thesaurus to standardize search terms and show relationships between terms. Given the size and volatility of the Internet, it is surprising that so many users do find the documents they want. Nevertheless, it is difficult to disagree with the conclusions of the NRENAISSANCE Committee on the effectiveness of Internet searching tools (1994, p. 63):

> Although some of these tools are proving very successful, they represent only a first step in the discovery of paradigms for the realization of on-line information. The Web pointers provide a way to navigate in cyberspace but do not provide an effective way to filter a set of objects based on selection criteria. In contrast, WAIS provides a way to filter through all the objects in a server but does not provide an easy way to link objects in different servers.
>
> As Paul Evan Peters of the Coalition for Networked Information observed in briefing the committee, we are in a paleoelectric information environment, with crude tools, hunters and gatherers, and incipient civilization, but more advanced civilization is coming.

Of course, improvements are being made daily. In the past we could safely assume that the Internet would be limited to WAIS, archie, and Gopher. In practice, all of these have already been replaced by a new generation of fast, sophisticated search engines, including Lycos, Yahoo!, HotBot, WebCrawler, and Alta Vista, to name but a few. Although these new search engines do not rely on authority control or cataloging, they do represent an enormous improvement in service. They also represent a threat. Librarians grew up in a world in which access methods had not undergone any dramatic changes since the invention of the card catalog. In half a decade, however, the Internet has gone from primitive search tools like archie to sophisticated search engines that will, in turn, be replaced by even more powerful search engines within a few years.

BIBLIOGRAPHIC CONTROL AND ELECTRONIC DOCUMENTS

Despite the availability of the Internet's browsing and searching tools, finding an individual document on the Net remains problematic. The Internet is so large that finding a particular document is "a daunting task" (Levine & Baroudi, 1993, p. 216). The magnitude of the problem can be better understood if we imagine a library with thousands of rooms "that has no card catalog, in which each shelf is arranged independently by the person who brought in the books on the shelf" (p. 216). To make the search more challenging, the "owner" of each file (book title) has the power to rename it at any time. There is, of course, no author control, so searching for all of the files owned by Johnny von Neumann would require to search for every possible variation in the author's name: for example, John von Neumann; J. von Neumann; Johnny von Neumann, Ph.D.

Subject access on the Internet is provided largely by individuals, and the basis for subject indexing is largely determined by personal interests and idiosyncrasies. Controlled vocabulary, thesauri, and index consistency are virtually nonexistent.

The magnificently vibrant and chaotic nature of the Internet extends even to the documents stored on it. The contents of the documents are, in a very real sense, also uncontrolled. For example, once we find the document we are looking for, we do not know if the text has been revised or edited. We may not even know if the author made the revisions. For example, when we searched for an article written by Brewster Kahle in 1991, we had no way of knowing if the article had been revised, edited, or updated by the author. The lack of authority control, the difficulty of finding individual articles, and the great value of the materials stored on the Internet have underlined the importance of asserting some type of control over the digital library.

Cataloging the Internet: Old Tools, New Problems

It comes as no surprise that some librarians viewed the Internet's bewildering and baffling jumble to be a splendid professional opportunity. By using the same powerful bibliographic control tools that organized the output of the printing press, librarians would once again perform their historic mission of preserving and organizing information for efficient access. A 1993 project sponsored by OCLC tested ". . . the suitability of current cataloging rules and record formats governing the creation of machine-readable cataloging records . . ." as a method of providing bibliographic control for the Internet (Dillon et al., 1993, p. 2). The study found that by "using existing record formats and cataloging rules, modified as necessary, libraries can begin immediately to provide improved description and access for an important segment of electronic information objects available via the Internet" (p. 36). The authors assert that "libraries stand ready today to begin or continue the process of providing bibliographic control for remotely accessed information objects" (p. 35). In fairness, it must be pointed out that the authors of this study did not plan to catalog everything on the Internet. Because the value of the information stored on the Internet varies so widely, ". . . the actual body of electronic files worthy of cataloging is rather small compared with the amount of information available" (p. 35). They conclude (p. 35):

While aspects of this electronic information collection—mutability, lack of fixity in a medium, remote accessibility—require adjustments in procedures for cataloging description and access, they do not argue for the abandonment of existing methods. To the contrary, the value of the nation's existing infrastructure of libraries, library systems, and local, regional, and national union catalogs must be leveraged for the information needs of the future.

The Inadequacy of the Old Cataloging Paradigm

This heroic, albeit ill-advised, effort to use MARC records to catalog the Internet illustrates how easy it is for experts in the old paradigm to persuade themselves that, with only a few minor modifications, we can resuscitate our old practices. Like the marvelously talented Swiss watchmakers, who believed that they needed only to refine their manufacturing processes to meet the challenge of the digital watch, many of our most talented technical service librarians cling to the hope that we need only make a few minor technical adjustments and then we will have mastered the challenges of ordering, accessing, and storing electronic documents.

While it would be comforting to believe that a few cosmetic alterations to USMARC will suffice to establish bibliographic control over electronic documents, conventional cataloging practices are simply not designed to work with electronic documents or, for that matter, in a networked information system. The conventional bibliographic record has, in the words of Thomas Peters (1991, p. 26):

> a strong bias toward the physical entity of the book over the intellectual content contained within the book. The basic unit for the catalog is not the text but the separate, bibliographically independent, publication.

Even the etymology of the phrase, "bibliographic control," unmistakably emphasizes that the "book" remains the central concern of cataloging practice. Unlike the book, electronic documents stored in a digital library are not unchanging, fixed entities. They are created, deleted, modified, moved, and copied at will. They have no container or independent physical existence. If we consider only the most obvious implications of this fact, it becomes apparent that storing information about the height of the electronic document (in centimeters, of course), LC call number, Dewey call number (used to shelve this incorporeal digital record), ISBN, edition, place of publication, publisher, and pagination makes little sense. Once again, the old rules of the paper-based paradigm fail when applied to digital data. It is difficult to disagree with De Gennaro that ". . . we need to develop new and imaginative ways" of dealing with the digital formats because the traditional cataloging rules and procedures are inadequate to deal with the new and fundamentally different electronic environment (1987, p. 34).

As we have noted, current cataloging practices emphasize the physical description of the information package—equally true for books, serials, film strips, video recordings, music scores, maps, and computer programs—not the intellectual content of the item being cataloged. Because of this emphasis on physical description, using the MARC record to access the Internet simply makes no sense because the current bibliographic records provide "completely inadequate representation of the subject matter dealt with" (Lancaster, 1991, p. 6). And, of course, subject access is precisely what Internet users need the most. Although it is easy, and increasingly fashionable, to poke fun at the MARC record's lack of subject information, we need to remember that the main purpose of cataloging has never been to provide access to the ideas contained in an individual book; the primary purpose has always been inventory control. Cataloging was designed to furnish a clear and detailed record of the library's most valuable asset: the collection (Lancaster, 1991). Nor need we denigrate or apologize for our profession's 2,000-year-old commitment to bibliographic control. The development of standard cataloging practices was a magnificent professional achievement that met the challenge of providing order and organization for the flood of texts that the printing press made possible. We must recognize, however, that we can no longer define access in terms of bibliographies or shelf locations; in the digital environment, *access* means access to ideas— that is, to the actual contents of a document.

Finally, "since libraries can barely afford to continue full-scale cataloging of traditional books and journals according to the current Anglo-American Cataloging Rules (AACR2), it is simply out of the question to extend those rules to a variety of complex electronic formats" (De Gennaro, 1987, p. 34). We must eventually concede that the professional challenge is not to repackage past solutions but to "explore and develop the ways and means of making information in electronic form a regular part of the library's collection and services" (De Gennaro, 1987, p. 31). The attempt to modify traditional cataloging practices to deal with the radically new electronic environment also demonstrates why "experience often becomes a liability rather than an asset" during paradigm shifts (Keen, 1991, p. 98).

The Perils of Incremental Change

Although it is normal to react to rapid change by fine-tuning the existing system, "incremental change will get you a ticket into day-to-day survival, but it won't get you a ticket for long-range survival" (McGill, 1986, p. 16). The problem with incremental change is that it frequently ignores the long-term potential of a new technology. As we saw when we looked at the case of vacuum tubes and transistors, the mature technology on which vacuum tubes are based was simply unable to keep up with the rapid improvements made in transistor performance.

Paper-based media, another mature technology, simply cannot match the dramatic advances made in digital media. For example, book preservation remains an enormously expensive and time-consuming undertaking, and no dramatic changes in the basic technology are expected. Using conventional methods of book preservation, the Library of Congress estimates that repairing the library's collection of rare books will keep the preservation department busy for the next 12,000 years (Weeks, 1991, p. 28).

By contrast, digital storage technology is continuing its explosive rate of development. Five years ago a PC hard drive's capacity was measured in megabytes. Today PCs routinely come with gigabyte hard drives. Admittedly, this increase in storage capacity does not address all the problems involved in converting paper documents to a digital format, but it does illustrate how the dramatic improvements in digital technology are driving down the costs of storing documents. Comparable improvements in OCR technology will soon reach the point where it will be cheaper to store the contents of a book on a CD than to restore the book. While rare books and art books are in no immediate danger of being replaced by CD-ROM copies, within the next five years, economic considerations will mandate that many old books be displaced by CD-ROM copies.

The cost of housing printed materials has made the switch to digital storage media increasingly attractive. As noted earlier, the Columbia Law Library found that it was more cost-effective to store materials in digital format than build a $20 million addition to the library. An even more dramatic example of the advantages offered by digital media as a storage medium is given by Ventura (1988), who notes that the documentation for an F-18 fighter filled 300,000 pages and required 58 cubic feet of storage space when printed. The same information stored on a CD-ROM used a mere .04 cubic feet.

If we look at the problem currently confronting the Library of Congress, we can get a better understanding of why Seiler and Surprenant argue that "it is already too expensive to maintain print collections and doubly so to duplicate print and electronically stored information" (1991, p. 30). The "prohibitive expense of maintaining books these days" is clearly summarized by Weeks' description of the shelving requirements faced by the Library of Congress (1991, pp. 13–16):

> The library has an insatiable appetite for more space, and for good reason. Consider these numbers: The library's collections of nearly 100 million items are stashed away on 532 miles of shelving. It has more than 20 million books and pamphlets. . . .
> Since the library adds 1.6 million items a year, the obvious question is where will it be stored. Can the library, in this age of financial constraints, keep spending millions of dollars each year to keep books alive, or will it focus its attention and budgets on the ever-evolving multimedia technology?

Like its U.S. counterpart, the new building for the French National Library (the Bibliotheque de France) is required because the old Bibliotheque Nationale cannot house the collection. By 1995 not one inch would be left of the Bibliotheque Nationale's 100 miles of shelf space (Higonnet, 1991, p. 32). Yet, the architectural design of the new national library, the Bibliotheque de France, was "a librarian's nightmare" (p. 32). In trying to understand the reasons for the selection of a design that was patently unsuited to house printed materials, Patrice Higonnet surmised (p. 32) that:

> It seems ... plausible to suppose the architects and managers of this devastating project simply think that books are on their way out. They may well believe that what once would have been in print will soon be electronified, microfilmed, and microfiched. In this view there will never be many books in the towers, and if there are and if they do decompose, it won't really matter because all those pages will be on CD-ROMs, on-line periodicals, and computer screens.

While librarians and book lovers everywhere reacted with dismay, it would seem that the architect was guilty of nothing more than assuming that information technology would dramatically change the way in which we understand the word "library."

THE PROFESSIONAL AGENDA

> There is a dangerous timelag built into even the most successful institutions. They are created at one time in response to some particular opportunity in a given historical context. And then as the context shifts, the institution finds itself carrying excess baggage that is no longer useful.
> —John Sculley

As librarians prepare to meet the challenges of the next millennium, they face a paradigm shift that may be even more profound than the changes triggered by Gutenberg's famous invention. Unquestionably, the profession will have much less time to understand and deal with the problems and opportunities created by the enormous power of the new information technologies. As a result, "We now face a critical juncture in our relationship with computer technology: we can allow it to shape the future role of libraries or we can pattern it to serve the chosen values of the profession" (Adams, 1988, p. 31).

In the ongoing debate over the role of technology and the future of the library, we have all too frequently lost sight of our professional values. Even our conception of a library has become blurred. On the one hand, we are warned by technophiles such as Robert Zich, the head of special projects for the Library of Congress, that we confront "a future in which libraries will be nothing more than museums of the printed word unless they seize the opportunity to become clearinghouses of electronic information" (Weeks, 1991, p. 30). On the other hand, some in our profession are determined to preserve our primary mission unchanged. There is the nagging conviction that we must remain first and foremost a book-filled library and that the high-technology world of digital information, CD-ROMs, and computer networks is not really fundamental—or even compatible—with our professional values (p. 13). As one uneasy staff member of the Library of Congress wistfully remarked about LC's multimedia American Memory project, "we are concerned that we're a library and maybe we shouldn't do this at all" (p. 13). These early concerns have only been exacerbated by the announcement that the Library of Congress intends to spend $13 million on this project over the next few years.

For this generation of librarians, the central issue is how to reinvent the library to make it a viable and thriving institution in the age of digital information while still carrying out its historic mission of preserving and disseminating the collective memory of our civilization. It is now apparent that information technology has made "new kinds of electronic 'libraries' or data banks necessary and possible, whether or when it will make Gutenberg-type libraries obsolete, nobody really knows" (De Gennaro, 1987, p. 69). What is clear, however, is the need for library professionals to redefine and, in a very real sense, reinvent the library by developing the "appropriate policies, strategies, and technologies for providing access to published as well as unpublished electronic files just as it now provides access to other (and frequently closely related) published and unpublished materials in paper formats" (p. 32).

LIBRARIES AND CULTURE: CLOSURE OR TRANSITION?

> The safest general characterization of the European philosophical tradition is that it consists of a series of footnotes to Plato.
> —Alfred North Whitehead, *Process and Reality*

In systems jargon the term "greenfield project" refers to a systems development project that starts with a clean slate. The term implies that there are no existing systems or functions that have to be accommodated by the new system. Since greenfield projects are free of external constraints, programmers are free to develop the new system without compromising its elegance or performance by making it compatible with an existing system. All too often the high-tech visions of the future library assume that we can jettison the past and start afresh. Although such visions can be quite seductive, as responsible professionals we cannot succumb to the notion that the sacrifice of 2,000 years of library history will magically make all past and current constraints disappear.

An important—perhaps even the central—part of our professional responsibility is to serve as the guardians of our intellectual and cultural heritage. Regardless of the advances made in information technology, librarians will continue to be responsible for acquiring, preserving, organizing, and making available "the records of human achievement" (De Gennaro, 1987, p. 63). Moreover, material published prior to 1980 is unlikely to be included in the digital library because of the cost of translating this material into a machine-readable format. As a result, one of the unintended side effects of assuming that a switch to electronic libraries will magically solve all of our problems is that we will lose access to virtually all materials published before 1980. Of course, the pre-1980 materials will still remain on the shelves, but access costs will further limit use in a digitized environment. In effect, human history and thought would begin in 1980 because information technology privileges digital documents. Consequently, unless the library happens to have an edition of, say, Plato's *Dialogues* in digital format, humanities students will not have ready access to his ideas because he will not be included in the electronic library's database.

If we look at a simpler example, OPACs, the implications of the transition from paper-based collections to electronic documents becomes clearer. Virtually all academic libraries have split collections; that is, only a fraction of their total collection is listed on the OPAC. The OPAC listing, thus, shows a collection that is biased toward monographs published after 1980—or whenever the library replaced its card catalog with an OPAC. The remainder of the collection can be accessed only by browsing or working through the now defunct card catalog. Since only a tiny percentage of the library users ever refer to the card catalog, the OPAC has had the unfortunate side effect of making a large part of the collection virtually invisible to all but a handful of dedicated scholars who understand the importance of checking the card catalog.

The situation will be even worse on the Internet and its successors because in a database environment, any item not stored in the database has, for all practical purposes, ceased to exist. For all users of electronic information systems, our electronic libraries will provide access only to materials translated into a digital format. In this scenario the library truly becomes the museum of the book. And those materials that have not been translated into an integrated digital system will be further marginalized and little used. Students, increasingly dependent upon electronic resources, will live in an intellectual world where human thought begins circa 1980.

Those comfortable with the emerging information era see this as both natural and trouble-free, and as Seiler and Suprenant (1991, p. 31) make clear:

> It is possible that in one hundred years almost no one will read the literature—books and journals—from the past because it will be obsolete in the electronic age and in the electronic medium. As a consequence, our present plans to convert as much as possible of our print heritage to digits might, for the most part be a waste of money.

But surely librarians will object to such a casual dismissal of the value of the historic fruits of the human intellect. Philosopher Margaret Archer sees this attitude as the early sign of the emergence of what she labels the "Fallacy of Amoral Objectivity," wherein the "high-tech hopefuls" imagine a world where "the cultural realm becomes subordinate to information technology" (1990, p. 111). This bias complacently endorses the notion that we can safely abandon the ethical, the human, foundations of our collective sense of identity as we enter the brave new world of "instrumental reason." Such an attitude, Archer insists, renders "ethics superflous," and it tends to promote a dangerous form of "moral agnosticism." She forcefully reminds us that the postindustrial utopians have a tendency to "conflate instrumental rationality with morality and technical advance with social progress. Librarians must remain ever vigilant to these reductionist arguments, and must be willing to protest the suggestion that the "rational" and the "best" are always the same. Simply put, we must insist that Plato and the other great thinkers throughout history remain central to our neverending search for the blueprint for a just society (Harris et al., 1998, p. 14).

Nevertheless, the foregoing discussion illustrates vividly the importance that a shift in core technologies can have for a profession's paradigmatic understanding of its mission in society. Postindustrial utopians like Seiler and Surprenant (1991) recognize the fundamental truth that the canonical foundations of Western civilization have never been viable information commodities and that there is little reason to think there will be a commercial market for such work in a digitized information marketplace. But recognizing this, they jump to the conclusion that such canonical work is thus obsolete and "worthless." Such a radical break with our society's commitment to its collective memory is unlikely, and librarians would be well advised to abandon such utopian fantasies and get on with the complicated and risky business of fulfilling their historic mission in these changing times (Peters, 1991, p. 28):

> The most important issue facing librarians is how to provide access to the growing volume of information in electronic form, while at the same time maintaining tradition book and journal collections and services and providing appropriate links between the two.

Thus, it would seem that professional librarians must consciously confront the task at hand. We must accept the heavy responsibility of transforming traditional libraries into institutions capable of responding to and meeting the needs of our clientele in the information era. In what Penniman (1992, pp. 40–41) calls the "paradox of change," libraries have no alternative:

> If we do nothing, we will change, but not as we wish. We are in a changing environment, and without adjustment, our institutions degrade. To survive we must adapt. To state the paradox simply: to remain as we are—that is, to remain vital we must change. If we don't change, we won't remain vital.

Like all paradigm shifts, the transition to the digital library will not be painless. Since no one knows the exact nature of the future library, librarians must create learning organizations committed to the belief that the only way to intelligently reinvent the library is through constant experimentation.

PLANNING FOR THE FUTURE

> One would have to be in an advanced state of denial not to recognize that the
> world we grew up in is going, going, gone.
> Of course, there are a lot of people in denial.
> —Ed Oakley and Doug Krug, *Enlightened Leadership*

By their very nature, libraries tend to be conservative institutions—more focused on the preserving the past than inventing the future. While this outlook is a natural one, it carries with it some serious disadvantages. According to McFarlan (1984, pp. 100–101), the rapid changes in the way in which information is packaged and disseminated will dramatically alter the structure of the information industry within the next few years. McFarlan (pp. 100–101) uses the following example to illustrate the risks and opportunities that new technologies such as videotext and cable services will pose for organizations in the information industry:

> No example is more striking than the situation confronting libraries. They have a 1,000-year-plus tradition of storing books made of parchment and wood pulp. Soaring materials costs, the advent of cheap microfiche and microfilm, expansion of computer data bases, and electronic links between libraries will make the research facility of the year 2000 unrecognizable from the large library of today. Those libraries that persist in spending 65% of their budget to keep aged wood pulp warm (and cool) will be irrelevant to the needs of their readers.

While librarians may accuse McFarlan of hyperbole, his basic point is indisputable; that is, that developments in information technology would change the way in which information is stored, organized, and delivered. Such basic changes to the core technology of the library makes it imperative that libraries invest their limited resources to create a library capable of meeting the needs of tomorrow (Belasco, 1991, p. 81). In practice, library budgets have emphasized using discretionary funding to buy additional materials for the collection. In special cases, such as when buying a new OPAC, they have set aside part of their budgets to pay for the purchase of a new system. Rarely, if ever, have libraries developed and funded a long-term strategy that closely meshes a library's mission, strategic plan, and information technology.

In a study of the way in which nonprofit institutions employ information technology, Te'eni and Speltz report that they could not find a single instance of a successful information system "that required the organization to conceive a long-range plan and create a dedicated mechanism for gathering data before using them" (1993, p. 90). The authors contend that two factors underlie this record of failure (p. 90):

> The first is a consistent lack of strategic or long-range planning around IS [information systems] and technology, whether as part of comprehensive long-range planning or

as a distinct area of management. As has been noted, IS are never really viewed as more than an add-on tool for basic operations and a distant resource for accomplishing the artistic mission of the institution. The second, related factor is the inability of even the largest cultural institutions to commit a substantial amount of funding or staff time to the development of IS either on an annual or long-range basis. As long as the IS functions at these institutions are underfunded and understaffed, their potential will never be understood or explored.

Undoubtedly, Te'eni and Speltz are correct in their contention that the lack of funding and long-range planning have both played a significant role in the failure of libraries to exploit fully the enormous potential of information technology. However, as is so often the case when dealing with IT, there are no simple answers. As we explore in the next section, there are many other barriers that must be surmounted before libraries can take full advantage of information technology's enormous potential.

INTEGRATING IT: THE CHALLENGE FOR THE NEXT DECADE

While the effective utilization of IT is already central to the long-term success of most organizations, most firms "are a long way from fully exploiting the strategic opportunities that information technology offers" (Emery, 1987, p. xi). Emery continues by noting that "the gap between practice and potential has probably never been greater, and the penalties for failing to narrow the gap are bound to grow" (p. xi). Although Emery is referring to business organizations, his comments are equally applicable to libraries. For example, Lancaster (1991, p. 4) conclude that "on the whole, the [library] profession has been neither imaginative nor innovative in its exploitation of technology."

In part, this failure can be attributed to the novelty of the technology, its complexity, and its constant evolution. A more fundamental problem, however, is that the difficulty of integrating information technology into an organization has been seriously underestimated. Like most organizations, libraries have been content "to use technology to mechanize old ways of doing business" (Hammer, 1990, p. 104). Keen argues that "many of the disappointments and problems of IT come from automating the *status quo* rather than rethinking, streamlining, and eliminating work" (1991, pp. 129–130). Michael S. Scott Morton, the director of the Management in the 1990s Research Program at MIT's Sloan School of Management, has stated that the most important management task of the 1990s is to reexamine all dimensions of our organizations in order to take advantage of the power of information technology (1991, p. 11). In particular, we have been slow to recognize that libraries are large, complex systems in which the technical, organizational, social, and cultural components are mutually interdependent. As a result, any change in any part of the system will have an immediate impact on the rest of the system.

Before a library can create information systems that fully exploit information technology, they must:

- Develop an organizational vision that can be used as a guide for aligning the technical and organizational strategies of the library;
- Recognize that the adoption, introduction, and diffusion of information technology into a library involves social, organizational, and technical change; and
- Recognize that implementation of IT is not a simple, straightforward process.

Once these basic steps have been taken, librarians will be ready to acquire the necessary infrastructure of communications, databases, software applications, and educated staff needed to integrate information technology into the daily operations of the library in order to accomplish the institution's goals and mission.

TOWARD THE 21ST CENTURY

> We need not stumble backward into the future, casting longing glances at what
> used to be; we can turn around and face a changed reality.
> It is, after all, a safer posture if you want to keep moving.
> —Charles Handy (1989)

As we enter the 21st century, we have no means of predicting the exact nature of the changes that libraries will undergo in the next decades. We do know, however, that our ability to integrate information technology into our libraries will be crucial to our long-term success or failure. We certainly have no guarantees that we will be successful in making the many changes needed to transform our 20th-century libraries into 21st-century information centers.

Confronted by an uncertain and unknowable future, organizational and library literatures are replete with well-intentioned warnings that "we must shape the future, not let it shape us, despite the tremendous changes in information technology in our lifetime" (Penniman, 1992, p. 40) and that our ultimate success or failure "will depend upon our own perceptiveness, intuition, integrity, and creativity" (Savage, 1990, p. 199).

Although there is much truth in such exhortations, we also know that "good intentions are no substitute for professional skills and organizational resources" (Keen, 1991, p. 221). What we need are guidelines that will help us think about the crucial problems that will confront us in the coming decades. Fortunately, such guidelines now exist. After more than a decade of research and experimentation in business organizations, we now have enough experience with integrating information technology into organizations to be able to specify a general outline of how to accomplish this formidable task. Admittedly, these guidelines are of a general nature and heavily dependent upon the organizational context. They are emphatically not simpleminded recipes that miraculously guarantee quick success if rigidly followed.

Some may hesitate to draw upon research based upon the private sector under the mistaken belief that the experiences of business organizations have no relevance for libraries. This notion, however, is mistaken, as Lauffer notes in the following (1984, p. xii):

> There is no reason why you can't learn from the experience of business. Nor is there a reason why you can't apply business concepts and practices where appropriate. Certainly we all do it in the areas of accounting, information management, and, interestingly, human relations training.

GUIDELINES FOR REINVENTING THE LIBRARY

> In a few years, libraries as we know them will start to disappear,
> and information will be found on "the Net."
> —Douglas E. Comer (1995)

With few exceptions, information technology has usually been described as an autonomous, almost primeval force of nature that will inevitably bring about wholesale organizational changes that will improve service, efficiency, and productivity. Research findings and practical experience, however, indicate that implementing IT into an organization is an enormously difficult and lengthy process; and that unless the technical changes are in alignment with the organization's vision, strategy, and organizational structure, there will be no significant improvements in organizational performance (Walton, 1989; Morton, 1991). This mutual interdependence of organizational culture, vision, strategy, organizational structure, and technology is another way of saying that libraries are large, complex systems in which any change to any part of the system will have an impact on the rest of the system. As John Gall correctly notes, in a large system, there is no way to "change just one thing" (1988, p. 158). In the systems approach, there are no quick fixes or painless solutions that will solve all of our problems. Creating a library equal to the challenges of the coming decades will require much more of us than simply buying a "turnkey" system and plugging it in.

Once we look at the integration of information technology into libraries from the systems perspective, it becomes obvious why a change in our core technologies so "often creates and demands immense organizational and human resource changes. It changes the nature of jobs and careers. IT planning without organizational planning is almost sure to fail" (Keen, 1991, p. 17).

Because IT will affect virtually every component of an organization, there is a growing consensus in management literature that organizations that are successful in meeting the challenges of insistent change will be organized, staffed, and managed quite differently from the traditional hierarchical organizations that we know so well.

The rest of this book is designed to provide a roadmap of the route we need to take to transform libraries into institutions that are capable of responding to the societal information needs of the postindustrial era. Although the journey appears to take us down many unfamiliar paths, we are convinced that not only is the journey necessary, but it is overdue. To pretend otherwise is, in the words of Handy, to pretend that nothing has changed and to "live in a garden of remembrance as if time had stood still" (1989, p. 23).

We begin this journey by looking at the importance of developing a new vision of what the new library will be like. We will see how this vision can, in turn, be used to unify the efforts needed to transform the library into an organization that uses continuous learning and experimentation to cope with rapid change.

4

Organizing for Change: The Need for the Learning Organization

We live in a time of such rapid change and growth of knowledge that only. . .
a person who continues to learn and inquire can hope to keep pace, let alone
play the role of guide.
—Nathan M. Pusey, President, Harvard University, *The Age of the Scholar*

He that will not apply new remedies must expect new evils;
for time is the greatest innovator.
—Francis Bacon, *Of Innovations*

LEARNING: A TOOL FOR SURVIVAL

A fad is something that everyone wants today and no one wants tomorrow.
—Anonymous

Zero-based budgets, MBO, matrix management, T-groups, PERT/CPM, participa-
tive management, quality circles, TQM—these are but a few of the magical
management formulas that have dominated popular management literature for the
past 50 years. Considering the faddish nature of management literature, it is
tempting to dismiss the learning organization as simply the latest in a long

51

procession of management fads that strut across the stage for their appointed hour, only to be replaced by a still newer managerial panacea. Such a view, however, overlooks what Weisbord (1987, p. 175) calls "the central fact of life for organizations": namely, that we now live in "world created by accelerating change, growing uncertainty, increasingly unpredictable global connections of economics, technology, and people." As a consequence of this rapidly changing environment, organizations "are going out of business every day because they have failed to adapt to it [change] or they have adapted too slowly" (Ackoff, 1981, p. 4). In their classic 1978 text on organizational learning, Argyris and Schön (p. 9) sum up both the need for creating learning organizations and the difficulties of building such organizations:

> We begin to suspect that there is no stable state awaiting us over the horizon. On the contrary, our very power to solve problems seems to multiply problems. As a result, our organizations live in economic, political, and technological environments which are predictably unstable. The requirement for organizational learning is not an occasional, sporadic phenomenon, but is continuous and endemic to our society.
>
> Nevertheless, it is not at all clear what it means for an organization to learn. Nor is it clear how we can enhance the capacity of organizations to learn.

Ulrich, von Glinow, and Jick (1993, p. 54) conclude that organizational learning has become the indispensable survival skill needed by both private and public organizations:

> In fact, learning in organizations matters more now than in the past, for three reasons: workforce competence, capacity for change, and competitiveness. We believe that the acquisition of competence, the ability to change, and the need to be competitive are critical success factors for any public or private organization. By enlarging its capacity to learn, the organization increases its chances of success on each of these dimensions.

"The critical issue facing most organizations," write McGill and Slocum (1994, p. 5), "is not what to change, but what and how to learn." The importance of organizational learning was given additional support by a study carried out by the Shell planning group. The survey examined the history of 30 companies that had been in business for more than 75 years. The planning group concluded that institutional learning—"the process whereby management teams change their shared mental models of their company"—was the one attribute shared by all of the successful companies in the survey (De Geus, 1988, p. 70). Despite the recognition of the strong relationship between organizational learning and success, at present few organizations are truly capable of learning from experience, as McGill and Slocum point out: "The learning organization is a new paradigm. It represents a fundamentally different mind-set about business. It is a radical departure in purpose, processes, and practices from what most managers believe about how to do business today" (1994, p. xi).

The truly revolutionary nature of the learning organization can best be seen by first looking at how a learning organization differs from the traditional, bureaucratic organization that has dominated management theory and practice for the past century.

KNOWING ORGANIZATIONS VS.
LEARNING ORGANIZATIONS

In a time of drastic change, it is the learners who inherit the future. The learned find themselves equipped to live in a world that no longer exists.
—Eric Hoffer

The classical organizational model, called by McGill and Slocum (1994) the "knowing organization," has had a long and distinguished pedigree that can be traced back in management literature to the writings of Max Weber and Frederick W. Taylor. The knowing organization is not only the oldest of organization models, but it also continues to be enormously successful. Its membership includes such luminaries as UPS, McDonald's, Walt Disney Corp., Blockbuster Video—and virtually all libraries.

The knowing organization is characterized by the belief that there is a single best way to do a job, manage employees, and structure an organization; furthermore, these organizations believe that they know the one best way, and this is why McGill and Slocum have labeled them as knowing. The most famous and visible of all knowing organizations is McDonald's. Its 13,000-plus stores exemplify the best of what a knowing organization has to offer: efficiency, predictability, and control in production and customer services (McGill & Slocum, 1993, pp. 68–69). The best way of preparing french fries or cleaning a grill has been discovered, codified, and then committed to the corporate memory in the form of policies, procedures, rules, and regulations that cover even the most minute details involved in running a restaurant. McDonald's "engineered in" knowledge by designing machines that make it virtually impossible to overcook hamburgers, underserve the amount of fries, or shortchange the customer. In short, the food at McDonald's can be prepared and served only in the way that McDonald's "knows" to be the best way (McGill & Slocum, 1994, p. 33). McDonald's massive operating manual, in fact, attempts to anticipate every conceivable eventuality that could occur when running a restaurant and then provide specific guidelines for handling the problem the McDonald's way (p. 30). Most of the time, in most of the restaurants, the operating manual covers most of the problems. But as McGill and Slocum note, when the environment poses an unanticipated problem, such as the irate mob that gathered in front of the Barcelona, Spain, McDonald's to protest the U.S. bombing of Libya in 1986, the manual may offer no advice. In that case, the owner prudently closed his restaurant and went home. That night the restaurant was firebombed—another event not covered by the manual (p. 32).

The characteristics of knowing organizations have changed little in the past century. They continue to emphasize efficiency as the true touchstone of organizational health. They remain focused on "standardized policies, procedures, rules, and regulations. The primary responsibility of management in a knowing organization is to control employees' behavior by enforcing the rules" (McGill & Slocum, 1993, p. 69). Not even customers are exempt from the knowing organization's rules, which is why "the food at McDonald's can be prepared and served only in the way that McDonald's knows to be the best way" (p. 33).

As long as the nature of the marketplace—the technology, customer expectations, and competition—remains relatively static, the knowing organization remains an effective form of organization. However, when the economic, political, and social environment enters an era of rapid change, the very strengths of the knowing organization—its high levels of conformity, routine, and risk-avoidance—become liabilities because it is these very attributes of knowing organizations that hamper their ability to learn from their own experience. They are, to use McGill and Slocum's (p. 70) evocative phrase, "learning disadvantaged."

Knowing organizations adapt to their environment by making incremental improvements to existing products, processes, services, and technologies. However, all of these changes are really only tweakings and fine tunings of what the organization already does. For example, McDonald's has reacted to the increasing concerns about fat in the diet, not by creating a radically new menu, but by announcing that its famous french fries are now fried in vegetable oil. At heart, the knowing organization remains incapable of fundamentally altering its operations because, in the words of McGill and Slocum "Real learning begins with an acknowledgment that managers don't know. A knowing organization would have to recant its very *raison d'être* in order to learn; few are prepared to be so bold" (1994, p. 36).

SINGLE-LOOP AND DOUBLE-LOOP LEARNING

> They know enough who know how to learn.
> —Henry Adams

Knowing organizations are also poorly designed to profit from experience. Their emphasis on efficiency, rules, and standardized procedures makes it difficult for them to process and learn from their experiences with their clients, suppliers, and staff. At first glance, the contention that knowing organizations, like large academic libraries, have difficulty in learning from experience appears to be an exaggeration of the facts. While it is true that large libraries are remarkably resistant to change, especially rapid change, they do, nevertheless, eventually adapt to their environment. During the last decade alone, for example, academic libraries have spent millions on purchasing CD-ROM products, OPACs, and the Internet in an effort to respond to their changing environment. It seems nonsensical to believe that their talented and well-educated library professionals are unable to learn from their experiences with clients, suppliers, and new technology.

Given these facts, why have so many management writers claimed that our traditional, rule-based organizations are learning-impaired? This seeming paradox can be resolved when we understand how organizational management theorists differentiate between single-loop and double-loop learning.

All organizational learning involves the detection and correction of errors. In single-loop learning, members of an organization respond to environmental changes by detecting and correcting errors, thus permitting the organization to carry on its current policies. "Double-loop learning occurs only when an error is detected and corrected in ways that involve the modification of an organization's underlying norms, policies, and objectives" (Argyris & Schön, 1978, pp. 2–3). Argyris and Schön (p. 3) report that their research demonstrated that most traditional organizations did "quite well in single-loop learning but have great difficulties in double-loop learning."

In other words, traditional organizations (McGill & Slocum's knowing organizations) can adapt to environmental changes as long as these changes remain within the ambit of existing organizational norms and culture. As a result, single-loop learning is primarily concerned with efficiency; that is, "with how best to achieve existing goals and objectives and how best to keep organizational performance within the range specified by existing norms" (Argyris & Schön, 1978, p. 21). When confronted with changes that require the organization to reexamine its underlying assumptions, goals, and mission, the traditional organization must shift to Argyris and Schön's double-loop learning—a type of learning that they are ill equipped to carry out.

While it is fashionable to disparage traditional, bureaucratic organizations as being learning-impaired, their reliance on single-loop learning allows them to accomplish some of their most vital functions, such as maintaining continuity, consistency, and stability (Argyris & Schön, 1978, pp. 122–123). Unfortunately, in a turbulent and rapidly changing environment, "organizations must be concerned with discontinuity, inconsistency, instability, and changes in the status quo" (p. 123).

DEFINING THE LEARNING ORGANIZATION

Wisdom is not the product of schooling but of the lifelong attempt to acquire it.
—Albert Einstein, *The Human Side*

Although management literature is replete with articles about "learning organizations" and "knowledge-creating companies," the concept of learning organizations "remains murky, confused, and difficult to penetrate" (Garvin, 1993, p. 78). In all too many cases, "the 'learning organization,' widely recognized as a strategic imperative, appears to be in danger of becoming more slogan than substance" (McGill & Slocum, 1994, p. 29). It is not enough to tell managers that they must build a learning organization based on systems thinking, ongoing dialogue, shared vision, and team learning. While these recommendations are indeed fundamental to building learning organizations, they do not, by themselves, provide a framework for action that managers can implement. They suffer, as David Garvin (1993, p. 79) notes, by being far too abstract and by leaving far too many questions unanswered.

Before we can create learning organizations, we need a well-grounded definition of learning organizations, one that is clear and easy to apply. We need clear guidelines that contain "operational advice rather than high aspirations" as well as "tools for assessing an organization's rate and level of learning to ensure that gains have in fact been made" (Garvin, 1993, p. 79). Garvin goes on to define the learning organization as follows: "A learning organization is an organization skilled at creating, acquiring, and transferring knowledge, and at modifying its behavior to reflect new knowledge and insights" (p. 80).

At the heart of this definition lies the recognition that if learning is to take place, new ideas are required in order to trigger organizational improvement. However, a true learning organization does more than generate new ideas"it is also "adept at translating new knowledge into new ways of behaving" (Garvin, 1993, p. 81). To institutionalize the learning process so that it occurs by design rather than by chance, Garvin (p. 81) argues that the members of a learning organization must be:

- Skilled in systematic problem solving;
- Committed to experimenting with new approaches and services;
- Dedicated to learning from the organization's own experience and history;
- Committed to learning from the experience and the best practices of others; and
- Proficient in transferring knowledge quickly and efficiently throughout the organization.

Most important of all, learning must become an integral part of the organizational culture and a value esteemed by its members. Before this step can be accomplished, all members of the organization must accept the need to unlearn and alter old (codified) patterns of behavior. This is a truly formidable task because it requires us to sacrifice the comfortable and accustomed routines that have served us so well in our traditional organizations.

Peter Senge, arguably the most influential writer on the learning organization, insists that the transformation of a bureaucratic organization into a learning organization requires far more than drawing new organization charts, reengineering old processes, or becoming customer-oriented. Although these are all important, even essential actions, the most important changes, in Senge's opinion, take place on an individual level; for unless individuals modify their behavior and thinking, organizational changes will remain superficial and transitory. Because of his emphasis on personal change, Senge identifies the following five disciplines as being necessary for the development and maintenance of a learning organization (1990, pp. 6–11):

1. Systems thinking;
2. Personal mastery, defined as the discipline of continually clarifying and deepening our personal vision;
3. Mental models, the pictures or images that influence how we understand the world and take action;
4. Building a shared vision of the future we want to create; and
5. Team learning.

Because large organizations are complex systems whose individual components interact with and influence one another, all five of these elements must be developed together. Ignoring any of them, Senge warns, will lead to failure (p. 12). The development of a learning organization must be carried out using a systems approach, for systems thinking provides the framework that integrates the five disciplines and "keeps them from being separate gimmicks or the latest organization change fads" (p. 12). Finally, Senge's five disciplines will not converge "to create *the* learning organization but rather a new wave of experimentation and advancement" (p. 11).

Unlike traditional bureaucratic organizations such as knowing organizations, the goal of the learning organization is not to create the ultimate, perfect enterprise that will flawlessly perform its functions with only minor and occasional adjustments. Learning organizations are driven by the recognition that the only means of coping with a rapidly changing environment is to create an organization that is capable of accelerated learning and (sometimes dramatic) change. Every accomplishment or failure opens new possibilities that require the true learning organization to continuously monitor and adapt its behavior. A learning organization will never achieve a perfect steady-state position; it will constantly be changing and adapting.

Perhaps the best way to understand the magnitude of the changes that must be accomplished to transform our traditional libraries into learning organizations is to specify the key attributes that a learning organization must possess. As the summary presented in Table 4.1 suggests, the creation of a learning organization has an impact on every major part of the library. Virtually every aspect of organizational life—including the attitudes and values of every employee—will be subject to change.

TABLE 4.1.
Attributes of a Learning Organization

A learning organization and culture are characterized by:
1.   A strategic intent to learn that features
   a.   a strong commitment to continuous experimentation;
   b.   learning as an everyday practice of the organization;
   c.   responsible risk taking; and
   d.   a willingness to learn from the past by acknowledging and learning from failures.
2.   Organization designs that facilitate learning through
   a.   permeable internal boundaries that encourage information flow among departments;
   b.   permeable external boundaries that encourage information flow from and to the
         environment;
   c.   flexible task alignment; and
   d.   network intimacy.
3.   Information and systems that promote a culture of openness with accurate and timely feedback.
4.   Rewards for learning that are both extrinsic and intrinsic.
5.   Mechanisms for learning from others that might include
   a.   alliances;
   b.   benchmarking; and
   c.   cross-functional teams.
6.   Learning leadership that.
   a.   models;
   b.   mentors;
   c.   manages learning; and
   d.   monitors results.

(Adapted from McGill & Slocum, 1993, p. 76, and 1994, p. 263)

ATTRIBUTES OF A LEARNING ORGANIZATION

Even a cursory look at Table 4.1 reveals that learning organizations are, in the words of McGill and Slocum (1994, p. 12),

> different in every way from organizations as we have known them. A smart organi-
> zation [learning organization] is distinguished from other organizations by the lead-
> ership, communications, and decision-making processes that it uses to learn from its
> experience and to purposefully alter subsequent experiences. Moreover, where nec-
> essary, the learning organization can alter the very way in which it processes its
> experiences with suppliers, customers, and competitors.

By definition, a learning organization must be committed to cultural values that encourage risk taking, foster experimentation, and promote learning and even a willingness to learn from mistakes. In fact, it is no exaggeration to state that a learning organization's strategy is predicated on a recognition that the only source of excellence is learning and that a commitment to continuous experimentation is the best means of institutionalizing learning (McGill and Slocum, 1994, p. 13).

This emphasis on experimentation and constant learning means that no single strategy or set of management practices can ever become the dominant and unchallenged credo. Since it is axiomatic that a learning organization is, by necessity, heavily dependent on accurate and timely information, learning organizations must develop information systems that add value to the decision-making process, deliver pertinent information (not massive outpourings), and is readily accessible to the people who need it (McGill and Slocum, 1994, pp. 14–15). Even the structural characteristics of learning organizations are affected by the need to collect, share, and disseminate information throughout the organization. For instance, learning organizations are characterized by highly permeable boundaries that allow the free flow of information between the organization and its environment. As a result, the genuine learning organization will be hypersensitive to environmental changes, including changes in client-centered information needs. One of the driving forces behind the urgency for establishing learning organizations is the awareness that the environmental context for information services is in an era of rapid and continuous change. Internally, information flow is enhanced by the blurring of the lines between management and employees, between departments, and between employees and customers (p. 14).

In a very real sense, the organization's structure is based on the need to enhance learning by putting the necessary information resources in the hands of the employees who need them (McGill and Slocum, (1993, p. 77).

THE HUMAN RESOURCE SYSTEM

> The illiterate of the year 2000 will not be the individual who cannot read and write,
> but the one who cannot learn, unlearn, and relearn.
> —Alvin Toffler

The human resource system is another area in which the learning organization differs greatly from the traditional organization in both purpose and methods. In particular, the ground rules for staff selection, training programs, reward systems, and leadership styles must be completely revised and rethought to meet the different needs of the learning organization.

To function effectively, a learning organization must recruit skilled, educated, and committed people who can thrive in a learning organization, with its learning culture, experimental approach to strategy, flexible structure, team learning, and encouragement of diversity. Most of all, a learning organization must select people not for what they know, but for their ability to learn (McGill & Slocum, 1993, p. 78). In the information age, "the most important skill that an employee has . . . is the ability to learn" (Crawford, 1991, p. 126).

Because learning organizations "cannot afford for their members to become obsolete through lack of continuing education," educational programs and staff training are no longer considered to be a peripheral activity, albeit a commendable one; instead, . . . in the modern business world employee training becomes paramount" (Davidow & Malone, 1993, p. 202). In the knowledge economy, the talented and committed employee has become more crucial to the organization's ultimate failure or success than any of the traditional assets, such as money, equipment, or physical plant. If this claim seems exaggerated, then we need only look at the case of Japan. Despite Japan's lack of raw materials, the country has become an economic powerhouse, primarily because of its high literacy rate and the development of a remarkably committed and skilled workforce (Crawford, 1991, pp. 24–25).

The reward system in the learning organization must also be modified to recognize and reinforce learning. This means that pay and promotion practices must be linked to team performance, risk taking, experimentation, and competency rather than on seniority or number of people supervised (Boyett & Conn, 1991, p. 135). The emphasis on risk taking and experimentation, which are absolutely essential for learning, also mean that

> punishments for failure and dissent are eliminated. In most organizations today, not only are risk-taking and dissent not encouraged, but they are severely punished and generally regarded by employees and managers alike as "career enders." By contrast, learning organizations encourage dissent.
>
> Unlearning the traditional response of denigrating dissent, and learning to encourage diversity for maximum learning, is one of the key challenges facing managers in learning organizations. (McGill & Slocum, 1993, p. 78)

LEADERSHIP IN A LEARNING ORGANIZATION

> A leader is best when people barely know that he exists. When his work is done, his aim fulfilled, they will all say, "We did it ourselves."
> —Lao-tzu

Leadership in a learning organization "poses a core dilemma for learning organizations" (Kofman & Senge, 1993, p. 18). Kofman & Senge continue by observing: that the "dilemma cannot be reconciled with traditional notions of hierarchical leaders being in control, for this implies that those below are not in control. It implies that the person higher in the organization is somehow a more important person."

In traditional organizations, it is assumed that the supervisor knows what all of his or her staff are doing. After all, one of the qualifications of being the boss is to know how to do everyone else's job. But in a learning organization, as Drucker (1993, p. 107) points out, the knowledge needed to perform a job is so specialized and so transient that no manager can fully understand the jobs of his subordinates. As a result, managerial authority can no longer be based on the assumption that managers make the decisions because they have the most expertise or knowledge. "In the old days when only a few people were well educated and 'in the know,' leadership," writes Harlan Cleveland (1991, p. 39), was based on command and control. In today's complex world, "the traditional modes of leadership, featuring 'recommendations up, orders down,'" simply does not work very well (p. 2). The knowledge worker cannot be led by diktat; instead, notes Cleveland (pp. 39–40) leadership is

> exercised mainly by persuasion, bringing into consultation those who are going to have to do something to make the decision work. Where people are educated and are not treated this way, they either balk at the decisions made or have to be dragooned by organized misinformation backed by brute force.

Leadership in a learning organization, thus, is a radical departure from the traditional view of the leader as an iron-willed autocrat who literally drags his or her organization along by force of personality. Leadership attributes in a learning organization are redefined as: communication skills; negotiating skills (for conflict resolution and consensus building); motivational skills; and change management skills (including trust-building skills, empowerment skills, and vision of the future) (Boyett & Conn, 1991, pp. 167–168).

THE CHALLENGE OF BUILDING A LEARNING ORGANIZATION

> To climb steep hills
> Requires slow pace at first.
> —William Shakespeare, *Henry VIII*

Despite the insouciant ease with which executives routinely announce that their organization is now a learning organization (McGill & Slocum, 1993, p. 78),

> the actual building and maintaining of a learning organization is a Herculean task. The demands of this task run counter to most of what is currently believed about managing organizations. Learning organizations must be willing to uncover their assumptions about themselves and their environment. Thus, organizational learning is about more than simply acquiring new knowledge and insights; it requires managers to unlearn old practices that have outlived their usefulness and discard ways of processing experiences that have worked in the past. Unlearning makes way for new experiences and new ways of experiencing. It is the necessary precursor to learning.

To create a true learning organization requires basic shifts in how people think and interact (Kofman & Senge, 1993, p. 5). These changes are so fundamental that they require the organization to reexamine and change many of its most basic cultural assumptions. Quite obviously, such fundamental changes cannot be achieved either by a display of good intentions or by giving the occasional motivational speech at staff meetings. Unless there is a deep personal commitment on the part of both management and staff, supported by adequate resources, a detailed training program, and a clear, shared vision, the efforts to foster a learning organization will be predestined to fail.

In the following chapters, we describe the processes and changes that are required to transform our current libraries into learning organizations. For reasons of simplicity and clarity, we have organized the remaining chapters around the basic tasks that must be accomplished if we want to transform our libraries into learning organizations.

Although the processes are discussed in separate chapters, we must remember that they are all interrelated and that each process is inherently iterative; that is, we cannot build a learning organization by following a sequence of 7 to 10 simple steps that, if faithfully followed, will guarantee success. The tasks are so interrelated and so overlapping that many of them must be carried out in parallel. Organizational life is simply too complex and too dependent on the contextual setting to ever be summarized by such a simplistic recipe. "Real learning," as Kofman and Senge (1993, p. 7) rightly observe, results in the development of new capabilities over time, "in a continuous cycle of theoretical action and practical conceptualization." Finally, we are attempting to describe cycles, loops, and spirals in a medium (a book) that, for all of its marvelous power, remains stubbornly linear.

5

Envisioning the Future: The Need for a Shared Vision

> If you don't know where you're going, any path will take you there.
> —Sioux proverb

> If you don't know where you're going, you might end up somewhere else.
> —Casey Stengel

ORGANIZATIONAL VISION

It was not until the late 1970s that "organizational vision" became part of the managerial lexicon (Kouzes & Posner, 1987, p. 83; Peters, 1992, p. 616). Prior to this, managers preferred to talk about mission or purpose, not vision. Within the space of a few years, organizational vision became one of the most ubiquitous terms in business literature. In 1989 *Fortune* magazine reported on a survey of nearly 900 senior executives from 20 countries; 98 percent of the survey respondents ranked vision as the top attribute needed by the CEO of tomorrow (Korn, 1989, p. 157).

The belated recognition by management theorists of the importance of organizational vision seems, at first glance, to be quite puzzling. Upon reflection, however, it becomes apparent that the emphasis placed on vision is yet another consequence of the rapid rate of change that organizations now confront. As recently as the 1950s, the rate of change was so sedate that organizational values, strategy, and products could be expected to last for a decade or more. Certainly, there was no urgent need for either corporations or libraries to worry about redefining themselves or their services because it was safe to assume that next year would closely resemble the current year. In such a relatively stable environment, the goal of management was to improve efficiency—to do what the organization had always done, only slightly better.

By the late 1970s, the pace of change had reached the point that most products and strategies had a life expectancy of only a few years. As a result, organizations, both for profit and nonprofit, found that planning meant more than extrapolating last year's trend lines into the new year. What was needed was an organization designed not for the status quo but for adaptability, innovation, and quick response. Such an innovative organization would be intensely customer-oriented, quality-conscious, highly innovative, and constantly improving (Peters, 1992, pp. 615–616). Strategic planners painfully learned that their rules-based control systems simply could not respond quickly enough to an environment that was in permanent transition. For organizations confronting discontinuous change, the traditional models of strategic management failed on two counts. First, they failed to lead the organization to reexamine its identity assumptions; and second, they underestimated the crucial role that shared meanings and values play in developing a common culture that allows independent action to be focused and collaborative (Limerick & Cunnington, 1993, pp. 136, 159–160).

Because there are no road maps or signposts showing the way to a viable future, organizations, like explorers, need a compass that will direct their efforts. The organizational vision, thus, serves as a kind of magnetic north that provides a stable reference point for strategic planning.

WHAT IS AN ORGANIZATIONAL VISION?

Every man takes the limits of his own field of vision for the limits of the world.
—Arthur Schopenhauer, *Studies on Pessimism*

An organizational vision is a statement about what we want our organization to become. It is a picture of the future we seek to create (Senge, 1990, p. 223). Ideally, the vision is a statement that conveys a simple-to-understand, compelling, and inspirational mental picture of where we want our organization to go and how we want to get there (Belasco, 1991, p. 104). An effective vision statement not only describes our future goals and mission but also communicates what the organization stands for and why each member of the organization should be committed to achieving this vision. Because one of the main purposes of the vision statement is to inspire employees and empower them to serve customers, the vision must have a strong emotional appeal; consequently, "an effective vision is neither a high-blown statement of philosophy, nor is it a bland 'mission statement' of what the company purports to do" (Quinn, 1992, p. 258). In other words, a vision is "a vivid picture of an ambitious, desirable future state that is connected to the customer and better in some important way than the current state" (Whiteley, 1991, p. 26).

It is also important to note that although the vision statement is closely related to strategic planning, vision is not a synonym for long-range planning (Whiteley, 1991, p. 27)

> Vision is a separate issue from strategy. An organization's strategy is like an architectural blueprint: a clearly drawn design that shows what must be done to achieve success. A vision is not a blueprint, rather it is more like an artist's rendering of a building under construction.

Nor should we conclude that a mission statement and a vision statement are equivalent terms. Granted, the two terms are closely linked, but management literature clearly distinguishes between them. The main difference is that mission statements, according to Robbins (1994, p. 12), "address the business that an institution is in, what an organization does, while vision statements express the motivation for that business." An organizational mission statement, thus, states the organization's purpose, not its direction.

While literally scores of definitions of the organizational vision have been proposed within the last decade, for our purposes we define the vision statement as a short, simple statement of some value-adding activity that positively distinguishes an organization in the minds of everyone with whom the organization interacts (customers, employees, stakeholders, suppliers) and provides a clear picture of what values the organization stands for (Belasco, 1991, p. 113; Whiteley, 1991, p. 27). Any effective vision statement, thus, must address at least the following points (Quinn, 1992, p. 258):

- What we do for the world (our mission);
- What we are best at (our core competency);
- Our basis of differentiation (our unique ability to add value); and
- The heart of our philosophy.

The most important function of an organizational vision is to state who we are and what we value. The vision statement, thus, establishes a context in which the more detailed strategy is developed as well as specifying the organization's relationship with its various stakeholder groups. A vision statement, thus, clarifies (Gerstein, 1987, pp. 37–38) the:

- Mission or purpose of the organization;
- Specific scope of the business in terms of its clients and the needs of the client group that the organization attempts to satisfy;
- Technology used to satisfy these customer needs;

- Enterprise's primary goals, generally expressed in terms of budgetary allocations, client-satisfaction objectives, and obligations to the library's stakeholders; and
- Organizational philosophy concerning the organization's position on key ethical issues, such as its behavior toward employees, clients, and other stakeholders.

THE IMPORTANCE OF AN ORGANIZATIONAL VISION

> Where there is no vision, the people perish.
> —*Proverbs 29:18*

Although organizational vision, like many other sensible ideas, has become so popular that it is in danger of becoming yet another in a long list of management fads, a well-conceived vision still remains "one of the most powerful tools a manager can wield in professional or creative services" (Quinn, 1992, p. 258). Vision, for Belasco, is "the difference between the long-term success of any organization and a certain second-rate position" (1991, p. 98). Burt Nanus (1992, p. 3) argues that "there is no more powerful engine driving an organization toward excellence and long-range success than an attractive, worthwhile, and achievable vision of the future. . . ." In their research on leadership, Kouzes and Posner (1987, p. 93) found that a clear vision had a significant impact on an organization; more specifically, they found, that "When leaders clearly articulated their vision for the organization, people reported significantly higher levels of job satisfaction, commitment, loyalty, esprit de corps, clarity of direction, pride, and productivity. It is quite evident that clearly articulated visions make a difference." For every organization trying to cope with a turbulent environment, "vision is not a luxury but a necessity; without it, workers drift in confusion or, worse, act at cross-purposes" (Nanus, 1992, p. 18).

Within the past few years, the library profession has also recognized that the vision statement is now a key component of strategic planning. In 1988 Judith Adams claimed that a well-articulated vision is essential to planning the future course of library automation (p. 31). A year later a group of influential academic library administrators (Woodsworth et al., p. 132) wrote:

> To influence the shape of libraries in the future, not only is it desirable to describe what the future should be—to outline a vision or an ideal—but doing so is a first step in ensuring that the vision becomes reality.

Robbins (1994, p. 14) is even more adamant in asserting that an organizational vision is an essential part of library strategic planning:

[I]t is clear that all organizations that achieve greatness are guided by a vision that is easily communicated and broadly shared among those who work for, or with, as well as use, the organization. An organization loses ground when a vision cannot be articulated for it, when its vision becomes cloudy, or when multiple differing visions come into conflict. Everyone associated with an organization needs to share in the organizational vision because vision forms the bond which holds any great organization together and supports its accomplishments.

Finally, in a 1992 issue of the *Library Journal*, David Penniman (p. 40), the former president of the Council on Library Resources, argues that "libraries are in jeopardy" because they lack the visionary leadership needed to describe the desired future and then make that future happen.

THE NEED FOR A SHARED VISION

No matter how high or how excellent technology may be and how much capital may be accumulated, unless the group of human beings which comprise the enterprise works together toward one unified goal, the enterprise is sure to go down the path of decline.
—Takashi Ishihara, *Cherry Blossoms and Robotics*

To be effective, the vision must be, in Peter Senge's phrase, a "shared vision" that acts as the organizational cement that focuses effort on a common goal (1990, p. 206). A shared vision connects and unites people together by building a collective sense "of what is important and why" (Senge et al., 1994, p. 299). A shared vision provides an alternative to interdepartmental squabbling and political infighting, are so pervasive in organizations. Senge claims that "without a genuine sense of common vision and values there is nothing to motivate people beyond self-interest" (1990, p. 275). Peter Drucker (1993, p. 53) makes the same point when he notes that without a clear, focused vision, members of an organization will substitute their local, departmental goals or define results in terms of their professional specialty rather than pursue the institution's overall goals. Joiner et al. (1994, p. 31) states that before interdepartmental barriers can be broken: "An organization must have a shared aim. Without a shared aim the elements of the organization have no guidepost by which to navigate. They operate as separate fiefdoms, each pulling in its own direction."

A shared vision is not only an antidote for dealing with suboptimizing problems—pursuing departmental goals instead of organizational goals—but it also serves as a potent means of unifying strategy and organizational culture (Hickman & Silva, 1984, p. 156). Because a shared vision emerges not from an executive ukase but from a coherent process of reflection and dialogue that is carried out at all levels of the organization and participated in by all of the employees, a shared vision has proven to be an enormously powerful means of developing a committed workforce that is dedicated to the purpose, values, and mission of the organization (Senge et al., 1994, p. 299). The truly shared vision binds people together by a common aspiration; employees are deeply committed to the vision because it reflects their own personal vision and values (Senge, 1990, p. 206).

According to Watkins and Marsick (1993, p. 195), it is impossible to create a learning organization without first developing a shared vision. They write:

> The learning organization begins with a shared vision. Learning is directed toward that vision. Learning organizations are not created by fiat, although it helps when executives embrace this idea publicly as a goal and make it policy. Instead, learning organizations depend on the participation of many individuals in a collective vision and on the release of the potential locked within them.

BUILDING A SHARED VISION

Building a shared vision, however, is neither easily nor quickly achieved. As Weisbord (1987, p. 337) wisely observes, the leap into new spaces "is never made in comfort." Creating a shared vision is inevitably accompanied by increased stress and anxiety. A tempting shortcut to the lengthy and arduous process of creating a shared vision is to rely on a visionary leader—a Thomas Watson, Sr., Bill Gates, Jack Welsh, or Bill Dix.

While there is no doubt that a visionary leader can bring about dramatic changes in a short period of time, the top-down approach to vision development has some serious limitations. Nadler and Tushman (1990, p. 94) rightly warn that charisma is, by itself, rarely sufficient to bring about lasting change in an organization. Leaders as successful as Jack Welch at General Electric and David Kearns at Xerox illustrate that even the most dynamic leaders cannot bring about lasting change by relying solely on their persuasiveness. While such visionary leaders are undoubtedly important catalysts in their organizations, it was these individuals successful creation of self-directed teams, learning systems, and streamlined management processes that provided the real foundation for bringing about lasting, large-scale change in General Electric and Xerox (p. 94).

THE IMPORTANCE OF A SHARED VISION

Although the glamour and allure of the charismatic leader make for inspirational reading, in practice "it is much better to develop a vision with others than to try to do it all on your own." Involving others in the development of the organizational vision, continues Nanus (1992, p. xix), is

> likely to improve the quality of your vision by bringing a wider range of informed viewpoints and expertise to bear on your search. It will be easier to implement the

results when your team has had a hand in the choice of vision and shares responsibility for it. And the search for a shared vision broadens everyone's understanding of the enterprise.

Since visions do not come with a guarantee, it is important that the vision be widely discussed, analyzed, and critiqued by many people from varied backgrounds. Such an ongoing dialogue presents the best, albeit imperfect, means of developing a practical, desirable, and empowering vision of the future (Senge et al., 1994, p. 24). According to Sims and Lorenzi (1992, p. 294), when the leader is the sole architect of the organizational vision, the employees tend to become "overly dependent on the leader" and "tend to flounder when the leader departs."

In most cases the creation of a vision turns out to be the easy part of developing a shared vision. Building commitment to a shared vision is far harder and far more time-consuming. As a result, it is common to see organizations prominently displaying their vision in public workspaces while their workforce remains either uncommitted to the vision or fails to understand how the organizational vision affects their jobs (Watkins & Marsick, 1993, p. 247).

Although building commitment is never easy, social scientists have known since Kurt Lewin's (1948, pp. 125–141; see also Wren, 1979, pp. 350–351) classic research that people are much more likely to change their attitudes and beliefs when they discover by themselves the need for change. Simply telling people or lecturing them about the need for change has consistently proven to be an ineffective means of changing beliefs.

If we apply this finding to building a shared vision, then it becomes obvious that "the key to gaining widespread, lasting commitment to a new vision . . . is to present the vision in such a way that people will want to participate and will freely choose to do so" (Nanus, 1992, p. 135). Thus, if an organization wants its people to become interested and active partners in the enterprise, then "the vision must be honestly discussed with them in terms that address their own legitimate concerns and feelings" (p. 135). In short, unless the vision development process is part of a genuine, ongoing dialogue that is widely shared and accepted throughout the organization, the vision statement runs the risk of being "little more than an empty dream" (p. 134).

EVOLVING VISIONS

By its very nature, the shared vision will never be a finished product; it will always be a part of a continuing process that seeks to orient the organization to the emerging realities of a changing world. Just as "visions do not leap out of our past wholly formed." (Kouzes & Posner, 1987, p. 95), a shared vision is neither static nor unchanging, which is why Nanus (1992, p. 32) emphasizes that vision formulation is an inherently dynamic process. Senge et al. (1994, p. 24) stress that the central tenet of the discipline of building shared visions is that "shared visions live in our ongoing conversations about what we seek together to create." Moreover, "a vision is not really shared unless it has staying power and [an] evolving life-force that lasts for years, propelling people through a continuous cycle of action, learning, and reflection" (Senge et al., 1994, p. 314).

According to Senge et al. (p. 314), a vital part of the process of building a shared vision is to use the process to act as a developmental tool that can be used to improve the listening capacity of top administrators as well as build the leadership capacities of the rest of the organization. Senge et al. (p. 315) conclude with a warning:

> Any organization which does not adopt a somewhat formal, concerted shared vision process will probably find itself following the path of least resistance. . . . The boss will gradually become more authoritarian, and the rest of the organization more passive.

VISION ENABLES LONG-TERM PLANNING AND EMPOWERS CHANGE

> If the mind has no fixed aim, it loses itself, for, as they say,
> to be everywhere is to be nowhere.
> —Michel de Montaigne, *The Essays of Montaigne*

A persuasive, clearly articulated vision remains the essential, indispensable part of any organization's long-term strategy. For many management-planning experts, the organizational vision has become the bedrock of the entire strategic planning process. Senge (1990, p. 210) argues that "it may simply not be possible to convince human beings rationally to take a long-term view." In fact, Senge (p. 210) contends that "in every instance where one finds a long-term view actually operating in human affairs, there is a long-term vision at work." Vision is now seen as an essential part of the change process. The linkage between change and vision is so strong that McGill (1986, p. 16) asserts that the only way to bring about "fundamental change is by creating new visions of the company, the organization, and its direction."

Vision becomes even more crucial when organizations confront the need to develop complex information technology systems. James Emery (1987, p. 263), a leading scholar in the areas of information technology and strategic planning, concludes that "lack of a shared vision inhibits the strategic use of information technology." Although information technology has the potential to bring about profound changes, "success will be elusive without some common understanding of what the organization wants to achieve . . . " (Emery, 1987, p. 263). Unless there is a shared vision in place, information technology "can never be more than an ad hoc and fragmented tactical resource" (Peter Keen, 1991, p. 32).

CRAFTING THE ORGANIZATIONAL VISION

I am captivated more by dreams of the future than by the history of the past.
—Thomas Jefferson

With the growing recognition of the importance of the vision statement, both profit and nonprofit organizations have set about creating an explicit vision that will provide direction for every employee. To date the results have not always met with success. Peter Senge (1994, p. 23) dismisses most of the alleged vision statements as being no more than a tiresome reiteration of yet another "motherhood and apple pie" statement of good intentions. Hamel and Prahalad (1994, p. 75) observe that "all too often the vision has been little more than a vaguely grandiose pronouncement of a leader who cannot distinguish between vanity and vision." No one more succinctly summarizes the real problem with vision statements than Richard C. Whiteley (1991, p. 21–22), who writes: "Even when managers declare that vision matters—even when they insist that it's vital, urgent, important—they seem incapable of creating one, or of making it seem real to the other people in their organizations."

Although it is not our purpose to write a text on how to create an organizational vision, we do need to know enough about the process to be aware of at least the basic steps involved in crafting a vision. For the most part, visions are crafted by asking questions about the fundamental purposes that an organization serves. Some of the most important questions are listed in the appendix.

LEADERSHIP RESPONSIBILITIES

Vision . . . is the foundation of leadership. Without a vision one cannot be a leader.
—J. H. Boyett and H. P. Conn (1991)

Although the questions in the appendix provide a solid foundation for creating a shared vision, library administrators must also worry about the balance between hope and anxiety. Do the library's employees and clients see the future as providing a challenge to improve the quality and range of their services or as a threat to the library's continued existence? If we attempt to escape the uncertainties of the future by allowing the urgent to drive out the important, the future will go largely unexplored, and ". . . the capacity to act, rather than the capacity to think and imagine, will become the sole measure of leadership" (Hamel & Prahalad, 1994, p. 5). Librarians will have failed to carry out their most critical professional responsibility of preparing for the future (p. 3) if they fail to:

- Scan the environment for new technologies that will improve the way in which we meet the needs of our clients;
- Spend time looking outward to see how the world could be different in five or 10 years; and
- Talk with our colleagues and clients to build a shared vision of the future.

No organization that thinks more about prolonging the past than about creating the future can expect to prosper in the coming decade, which is why the preceding questions touch upon the central issue in librarianship: Are we devoting too much energy to preserving the past and not enough to creating the future?

Unfortunately, we lack reliable data on how much time library administrators devote to preparing for the future. However, if we make the reasonable assumption that library leaders spend about the same amount of time on planning for the future as their business counterparts do, then we can use Hamel and Prahalad's research. Hamel and Prahalad (1994, p. 4) found that, on average, senior managers devoted less than 3 percent of their energy to building a corporate perspective on the future. In many companies, the figure is less than 1 percent.

According to these estimates, top managers spend, at most, an hour or two a week thinking about such difficult questions as: What new core competencies do we need to build? What new products and services should we offer? What new networked alliances do we need to form? and What new development programs should we fund? These are not easy questions; certainly, they are questions that take "substantial and sustained intellectual energy" (Hamel & Prahalad 1994, p. 4). Hamel and Prahalad (p. 4) argue that these questions have gone unanswered for the following reasons:

> They have received too little attention not because senior managers are lazy; most are working harder than ever. It is not even the sheer, bloody, time-consuming difficulty of answering these questions that scares top teams off. These questions go unanswered because to address them senior mangers must first admit, to themselves and to their company's employees, that they are less than fully in control of their company's future. They must admit that what they know today—the knowledge and experience that justify their position in the corporate pecking order—may be irrelevant or wrong-headed for the future.

COMMUNICATE THE VISION

> The meaning of a communication is the response that it elicits.
> —R. Bandler and J. Grinder

It is not enough to create a vision of the future. To make the vision effective, it must be shared across the organization, which means communicating the vision to others in a way that is exciting and persuasive (Boyett & Conn, 1991, p. 152). Perhaps no other stage in crafting a shared organizational vision is as difficult or uncertain as this one.

Since there is no magical recipe for communicating the vision, most of the management literature on crafting a vision either ignores this stage or relies on listing commonsense guidelines. For instance, Belasco (1991, p. 47) recommends that the organization establish regular communication channels for discussing the vision, encourage each employee to take responsibility for executing the vision in his or her area, and talk about the vision constantly. Senge et al. (1994, pp. 315–326) identify several different ways of communicating the vision:

- Telling: Boss tells employees what the new vision will be;
- Selling: Leadership tries to sell the vision to as many employees as possible;
- Testing: Leadership deploys the vision and sees if employees commit to it;
- Consulting: Leadership asks employees to recommend visions; and
- Co-creation: In an extended dialogue employees align their personal visions with the shared vision.

Depending on the culture and the health of the organization and the interpersonal skills of the workforce, each of these approaches has advantages and disadvantages. For instance, telling the vision may be necessary if the organization faces a serious crisis. On the other hand, telling people about the official vision does not guarantee that they will commit to it. A less obvious but equally serious problem is that research on verbal communication shows that people remember only about 25 percent of a message. Even worse, they may all remember a different 25 percent (Senge et al., 1994, p. 317). At the other end of the spectrum, co-creation recognizes the importance of having people work for what they want to build rather than to please a boss (p. 322). On the other hand, co-creating the vision requires a large investment in time and effort. It also requires that the employees have the interpersonal skills needed to carry on an extended dialogue among themselves.

Whatever approach is taken, the only certainty is that communicating the vision is an ongoing task that demands the constant attention of top management. Since the purpose of communicating the vision is to gain (or earn) the commitment of the organization's people, there are some approaches that are guaranteed to fail. One of the more interesting ways of communicating the vision to the workforce is used by a large aerospace company. This company, which shall remain nameless, created a magnificent and exciting vision. This inspiring vision was then printed on cards, which were given to each employee. Each employee was required to carry a copy of the vision statement when at work. In fact, any employee who could not show his or her copy of the vision statement when asked for it is subject to disciplinary action. In a bizarre fashion, this firm's direct approach solved the problem of disseminating the vision to every employee. Unfortunately for this corporation, dissemination did not guarantee either communication or commitment.

BUILDING COMMITMENT TO THE VISION

Only a committed workforce can transform the shared vision into reality. Without a high level of commitment, even the most inspiring vision is no more than just a piece of paper. Building commitment to the organizational vision remains one of the key responsibilities of top management.

The usual advice is to reward and recognize performance that supports the vision. This means that management must empower people to use the vision by identifying the areas that are most important to achieving the vision. When possible, we need to develop quantitative measures that we can use to measure or estimate how much progress we have made towards our vision. Senge et al. (1994, pp. 345–346) warn that the measurements must not be unilaterally imposed on the workforce:

> The measurements are not prescriptive; the senior manager does not impose them on the team. The team develops them for themselves, searching for the most meaningful priorities. . . . Once the team has agreed upon a set of strategic priorities, they have a set of milestones that can be used to mark their progress. They can conduct experiments to see if they can move closer to their goals, using the milestones to measure their effectiveness.

By tightly linking the vision to each employee's job, providing timely feedback, and rewarding behavior that supports the vision, the shared vision becomes more than just a platitudinous slogan. It becomes an understandable and attainable goal that is relevant to each person's job.

INTEGRATION OF VISION, STRATEGY, VALUES, AND CULTURE

The vision should also play a role in hiring practices. Belasco (1991, p. 176) recommends that organizations recruit and select people who will believe in and support the vision. It is vital that the organizational culture also be congruent with the vision. Since changing an organizational culture is an inherently time-consuming and enormously difficult process, it makes sense to avoid a head-on collision with the traditional organizational culture and values. Rather than directly challenge organizational values, the prudent leader will emphasize those existing organizational values that are consistent with the organizational vision and deemphasize those that are contradictory. Since organizations often hold many conflicting values at any given time, the very act of stating a new vision tends to strengthen some values and make others seem less appropriate (Nanus, 1992, p. 147).

MONITORING THE VISION

Although frequently overlooked, evaluating the performance of the shared vision remains a critical step in developing an organizational vision. Without some means of evaluating the vision, we will have no way of knowing if the vision is successful. Senge et al. (1994, p. 345) recommend that four or five specific goals be identified as strategic priorities that can act as measures of success for the vision. These measurable items are an essential part of the vision-creating process because they provide practical, concrete milestones that we can use to evaluate the organization's progress. Belasco (1991, p. 159) recommends that the people closest to the job be asked to come up with specific measures that are based on the organization's strategic priorities. These measures not only tell people how well they are doing but provide immediate feedback they can use to improve their performance.

In addition to developing specific measures, we can track the vision's progress by asking the following questions (Nanus, 1992, p. 160):

- Is the rate of progress satisfactory? Are enough changes being made?
- Are people acting as if the vision were their own? Are they taking the initiative and attempting to achieve the vision?
- Are the organization's goals, structures, processes, reward systems, and policies consistent with the vision?
- Are influential leaders championing the vision?
- Is the organizational culture supportive of the vision? Is it moving toward a closer alignment with the vision?
- Has the organization been innovative enough in implementing the vision?

The final test of vision—and in some ways the most important test—checks to see how well the vision matches our personal values. Is the vision honestly based on the governing values and beliefs of the members of the organization? The set of governing values might include how we behave with our fellow workers, how we regard our customers and community, and the lines that we do not cross (Senge et al., 1994, p. 302). The importance of aligning our personal values with the organizational vision is clearly summarized in the *The Fifth Discipline Fieldbook* (p. 302):

> When values are articulated but ignored, an important part of the shared vision effort is shut away. By contrast, when values are made a central part of the organization's shared vision effort, and put out in full view, they become like a figurehead on a ship: a guiding symbol of the behavior that will help people move toward the vision. It becomes easier to speak honestly, or to reveal information, when people know that these are aspects of agreed-upon values.

LIBRARY VISIONS

Like M. Jourdain, who did not know he had been speaking in prose for more than 40 years, many of our venerable institutions had strong, pervasive visions centuries before the notion of organizational vision became popular. Certainly this is true of libraries, which have operated off a well-developed, albeit rarely articulated vision of their role in society. Within the last 30 years, the traditional library vision has been challenged, modified, and decried. Nevertheless, the traditional library vision, despite its increasing senescence, underlies the mental models that library professionals still use to define the purpose of the library, the importance of the collection, and the role of the librarian. In the next chapter, we analyze the traditional library vision, discuss its limitations, and argue that if libraries are to survive in the information age, they must develop a new vision that is client-centered rather than collection centered.

APPENDIX:
CRAFTING THE VISION:
ASKING THE CRITICAL QUESTIONS

Strategic Context of the Library: External Focus
(Adapted from Hickman & Silva, 1984; Senge et al., 1994)

1. What are the critical success factors for the library?
2. What are the most important trends in the information industry?
3. What kind of image does our organization have?
4. What is our unique service?
5. What is our unique competitive advantage?
6. How are we funded?
7. Is our future secure? What have we done to ensure our future?
8. What role does the library play in the community?
9. What is the critical technology that is driving the information industry?
10. What have been our major successes in the past decade?
11. What have been our major failures in the past decade?

After answering each of these questions, we need to ask ourselves how we would want to change these answers in five years.

Strategic Context of the Library: Internal Focus
(Adapted from Hickman & Silva, 1984; Senge et al., 1994)

1. Who are the key stakeholders within our library?
2. Who are the key stakeholders outside the library?
3. What changes are taking place among our stakeholders?

4. In what ways does our library empower people?
5. In what aspects does it disempower them?
6. How is our strategic plan used?
7. What special skills do we offer to our clients?
8. What special skills will we need in five years?
9. How do our employees feel about who we are?
10. What are our values?
11. How do we treat our staff?
12. How do we recognize excellence?

Strategic Context of the Library: Client Focus
(Adapted from Burrus & Gittines, 1993; Hickman & Silva, 1984)

1. How do we improve the quality of life for our clients?
2. How do we add value for our clients?
3. How effectively do we compete?
4. What do our clients really want?
5. What value do our clients place on our services?
6. In what ways are our information services distinctive and unique?
7. What would we do if we had an unlimited library budget?
8. Are we doing the same things we did a year ago? Two years ago?
9. In what significant ways has our professional expertise changed in the last five years?

Strategic Context of the Library: Management Focus
(Adapted from Hamel & Prahalad, 1994; Hickman & Silva, 1984)

1. Do the senior administrators have a common vision of how the information industry will be different in 10 years?
2. Is the library's vision of the future reflected in its short-term priorities?
3. How influential is the library community in setting the rules of competition in its industry?
4. Are we leaders in defining new ways of doing business?
5. Are we leaders in setting new standards of customer satisfaction?
6. Are we more concerned with protecting the status quo than with reinventing the library?
7. Are our leaders aware of the dangers posed by new technologies?
8. Is the library pursuing new opportunities with as much passion as it is pursuing operational efficiency?
9. Are we driven by our view of future opportunities or by the need to protect traditional library operations?

6

Libraries and the Monumental Weight of History: Old Visions, New Challenges

> Historic continuity with the past is not a duty, it is only a necessity.
> —Oliver Wendell Holmes, Jr.

TRADITIONAL LIBRARY VISION

Because an organizational vision has become so fashionable, it is rare to find an institution that does not have an official "vision." It is almost as rare to find an organization that has a genuine shared vision that truly represents the aspirations and hopes of its members, and rarer still to find an organization that has stated in its vision how the organization will act to add value for its clients. Certainly libraries have not shown any special aptitude for avoiding the vague, fluffy, nebulous vision statement. In one respect this failure seems odd, for librarians have been committed for centuries to a surprisingly clear and comprehensive vision of themselves and their institution. In fact, this vision remains a powerful influence on library operations and a clear example why we need to heed Moshe F. Rubinstein's (1986, p. 61) advice to look to the past when planning the future:

> When we are preoccupied with predictions for what the future holds in a particular field, it helps to go back to lessons of history and probe the genesis of past

79

developments. This is in the nature of a mixed-scanning approach with a holistic view of many fields and developments, and detailed probing of one field or development. It can help us identify connections between fields and developments that on first sight appear vastly unrelated.

Since it is easier learn about creating our future if we know where we have come from, we need to consider in this chapter the following questions, which are loosely adapted from *The Fifth Discipline Fieldbook*, (Senge et al., 1994, pp. 341–343):

- What was the original vision and purpose of the library?
- What traditional roles and functions have libraries performed for us?
- What were the major milestones in the library's life, relative to its original purpose?
- Has the library's original sense of purpose changed?
- When did that change take place?
- What caused the change?
- Was the change a creative effort to embrace new opportunities or a reactive change forced by events?
- What parts of the original purpose remain viable?
- What parts of the original vision need to be rethought?

In the traditional library vision, the collection is the most important part of the library. Historically, librarians have, since the time of the Alexandrian Library, wholeheartedly embraced the dictum that the larger the collection, the better the library. Underlying this vision is the belief that books are important; in fact, books are so important in this view that we need to collect all of them so that not one single page or idea is lost to posterity. This vision, of course, emphasizes the role of the library as the intellectual custodian and warehouse of our civilization.

This vision, which we call the "traditional vision," has had such a powerful appeal that it has become one of the great unquestioned tenets of librarianship. In a very real sense, it has defined the role of the professional librarian as a servant of the collection. Because of the central importance of the collection in the traditional vision, the professional librarian's highest duty is to collect, store, and preserve as much material as possible. The practical reasons for this emphasis on increasing and protecting the collection are often forgotten. It harks back to a time when books were virtually the only means of storing information beyond the life expectancy of an individual and a rare and expensive commodity. By assiduously collecting and preserving these valuable artifacts, librarians added enormous value for their users and society in general. Since the collection was how the library added value for its users, the collection, not the librarian, was seen as the ultimate justification for the library's existence. As a natural outgrowth of the traditional vision's emphasis on the size of the collection, the acquisition of new materials became the primary task of the great scholar/librarians of the 19th and early 20th centuries (Harris & Hannah, 1996).

In a popular variation on the traditional library vision, libraries serve society by acting as a powerful force for "culturally uplifting" the masses. In this particular vision, librarians believed so strongly in the power of the printed word that they felt that reading could transform the masses. Books, especially the classics, were considered a powerful change agent that would bring culture and decorum to the masses. Implicit in this view was the notion that, if available, the canon would be read; and if read, the great books would change the reader. Once again, books, especially high-culture books, remained the raison d'être of libraries.

LIMITATIONS OF THE "LIBRARY AS WAREHOUSE" VIEW

> Look before, or you'll find yourself behind.
> —Benjamin Franklin

The library as repository and protector of our intellectual heritage is an enormously persuasive vision. The image of the library (and librarian) as the defender and preserver of the greatest ideas even put on paper has an aesthetic appeal that is well-nigh irresistible. This view of the library is the origin of many of the library profession's most esteemed cultural values. Unfortunately, the reaction of many dedicated librarians to the challenges of the digital age is to see themselves as the defenders of all that is best and noblest in our past. While the role of preservation remains an important one for national libraries, the visceral appeal of this position has caused many otherwise intelligent professionals to view any attempt to give equal preference to digital information as the worst type of professional apostasy or treason.

While no one can seriously question that preservation of our intellectual and cultural heritage remains an essential role for libraries, it is a role reserved for only a select few of the very largest libraries. Undoubtedly, a compelling case can be made for preserving the collections of the British Museum, the Library of Congress, and France's Bibliothéque Nationale—to name only a few of the great research libraries—but how many of us would want to defend the budget request for the local public library or even a university library by claiming that we are defending civilization?

Paradoxically, this noble vision of the library as the repository of all that is best in our thinking and writing threatens the continued existence of the library as a vibrant and evolving institution ready to continue to meet the needs of its customers. It is, sadly, an example of Burt Nanus's (1992, p. 157) observation on the impermanence of even the grandest vision:

Nothing is more common than a vision that has overstayed its welcome. Every leader wants an enduring vision, so once the organization is committed to it, all energies can be invested in its fulfillment. But although a vision may be the right one at the time it is formulated, rarely is it right for all time. The world changes, and so must the vision.

Consequences of Traditional Vision

If a collection-centered view of the library is adopted, then the library's focus is on internal operations—not the needs of the public. The warehouse view may, in part, explain why library patrons so often feel that libraries are designed to meet the needs of librarians and not the needs of the library's clients. The library's customers are right in one respect, in assuming that many of the library's rules and procedures were not designed to meet their needs. However, they are wrong in thinking that the rules were created to benefit librarians. In most cases the rules were designed to protect and preserve the collection—not benefit the librarians.

The way in which academic libraries select monographs offers us a classic example of how libraries privilege collection needs over customer needs. Unless a volume is ordered through an automatic vendor program, the title will be ordered only after the monograph has been reviewed. By waiting for the reviews, the library increases its probability of adding only quality materials to the collection. In other words, the need to safeguard the quality of the collection outweighs the patron's need to get the material as quickly as possible. What makes this decision even more revealing is that library studies have repeatedly shown that over half of the uses of a monograph typically occur during the first year after a book is published.

The needs of the collection are also at least partially responsible for our splitting the serials collection into multiple fragments. Academic libraries routinely subdivide the serials collection into bound and current periodicals; and, of course, the indexes to the serials collection are stored in yet another place in the library. Admittedly, librarians have logical reasons for fragmenting the serials collection in this fashion. Housing bound and unbound serials in separate locations simplifies shelving and maintenance. On the other hand, splitting the serials collections and its indexes causes serious problems for the library's clients. Most revealing of all, the problem of using the serials collection is seldom discussed or debated. With few exceptions, librarians instinctively and, for the most part, unreflectively, trade off user convenience anytime it conflicts with the need of the collection. If we were really client-centered, would we sacrifice customer convenience with so little thought?

LIBRARY: SOURCE OF LAST RESORT

In a famous editorial, C. N. Mooers (1960, p. ii) points out that an information system—however well devised—will not be used if ". . . it is more painful and troublesome to have information than not to have it." Unfortunately, for many of the library's reluctant clients, the library is frequently seen as both painful and troublesome to use. As William J. Paisley (1968, p. 9) notes, "The levels of frustration in using libraries are awfully high for most people . . . " It is a place where "you almost have to drag something out of" (unnamed librarian quoted in Paisley, 1968, p. 18).

Maurine Pastine (1987, p. 173) observes: "For many, the library is the last place one goes to get information." Although retrospective materials, literary texts, and bibliographies are often reverently spoken of by librarians, they are seldom used. Pastine concludes that instead of using the library, most "poets, philosophers, artists, musicians, novelists, and other humanists have relied on their own files and their colleagues to provide needed literature citations. . . ."

Even more curious, faculty members, who are seemingly the natural clients of the academic library, have been found in study after study to avoid using libraries in their research. In a three-year study of scholarly communication, researchers concluded that scholars, by a large majority, prefer to use their own personal collections (National Enquiry into Scholarly Communication, 1979, pp. 133, 135; see also Miller, 1986). Rudd and Rudd (1986, p. 319) found that both faculty and students sought to avoid information overload "by either avoiding the library or, once in the library, spending little time in the information search and giving up quickly."

EASE OF ACCESS

A more popular reason for explaining why so many potential clients avoid using the library is ease of use. There is a large body or research that indicates that "information sources tend to be chosen on the basis of perceived ease of use, rather than on the basis of the amount of information expected from the source" (Salsin & Cedar, 1986, p. 113; see also Gerstenberger & Allen, 1968, pp. 275–276). In their study of engineers, Salsin and Cedar found that accessibility and ease of use are stronger predictors of usage than is technical quality.

This information-seeking behavior is so pervasive that it has been honored with a name: The Principle of Least Effort (Bates, 1986, p. 374). According to Thomas Mann (1993, p. 91), this principle states that

> most researchers (even "serious" scholars) will tend to choose easily available information sources, even when they are objectively of low quality, and, further, will tend to be satisfied with whatever can be found easily in preference to pursuing higher-quality sources whose use would require a greater expenditure of effort.

Based on his review of the literature concerning information-seeking behavior, Mann (1993, pp. 97–98) concludes:

Given a choice between a system of access to information that is perceived as easy to use and one that is perceived as difficult, nearly all researchers will choose the easy path alone, regardless of the fact that it may offer lower-quality content.

LIBRARIANS FOR QUALITY: ECHOES OF HIGH CULTURE VS. CUSTOMER ORIENTATION

> No place affords a more striking conviction of the vanity of human hopes
> than a public library.
> —Dr. Samuel Johnson

As might be expected, the Principle of Least Effort has posed a dilemma for many practicing librarians. Convenient, quick online systems such as *InfoTrac* have proven to be enormously popular with the library's customers; however, librarians worry because the online systems tempt users to ignore the rest of the library's resources. Harter and Jackson (1988, p. 525) summarize these concerns as follows:

> [R]eference librarians are obligated to ensure that users are given the opportunity to retrieve, either independently or with the help of a librarian, relevant and high quality information related to their needs. We cannot abdicate this responsibility even though, at times users may opt for convenience because of their lack of knowledge about the art of the possible. . . . Our goal should be to provide high quality information services.

Librarians' duty to persuade (coerce?) their clients to use the "best" sources is yet another example of how the traditional vision continues to dominate our professional thinking. It also illustrates that the traditional vision is emphatically not customer-oriented. In fact, the traditional vision, in its high-culture variation, is definitely not in favor of pandering to the masses, as the following passage makes clear (Van Arsdale & Ostrye, 1986, p. 515):

> The concept of introducing an attractive and easy-to-use, but limited, searching tool into the undergraduate environment must be seriously addressed. Students may be eager to use the automated system, but they appear to have dropped efforts at more traditional searching and assumed that their electronic search will suffice. Our reference staff encouraged many students to pursue their research in other, more comprehensive sources, but few students did so. Typically, the undergraduate user prints out whatever results from the search term . . . and thinks the topic has been fully researched. The system encourages little or no judgment on the part of the student to select or use the information provided, an unfortunate consequence of most automated systems. . . . The authors find it difficult to provide a service because it is popular.

As this passage indicates, librarians assume that only they know how to use the library correctly. Since the reference staff assumes that the library's customers do not know what is best for them, it becomes the duty of the librarian to decide what each customer needs. This view of the librarian as dispenser of wisdom to the terminally inept may be professionally flattering; however, condescension has never been an effective means of building good customer relations. Even worse, there is little evidence that librarians are knowledgeable about customer needs. Their area of expertise is the organization and storage of information—not the assessment of customer needs. For instance, if a client needs only two or three current articles on a topic, we have no right to claim that the customer does not know how to use the library simply because he or she ignored hundreds of other articles on the same topic. Most information seeking "is discretionary. Because of this, users often have little or no reason to persist in using systems that are 'unfriendly'" (Wilberly & Dougherty, 1988, p. 150).

Even more important, if clients consistently fail to retrieve the materials they need for their research, librarians should not automatically assume that the clients are at fault. Perhaps the real fault lies not with a customer's limited cognitive abilities but with the traditional collection-centered organization of materials that makes it simply too difficult and time-consuming for the average customer to find relevant materials. Perhaps the library's reluctant clients have solid reasons for considering the library to be the information source of last resort.

There is considerable evidence that people avoid using the library because the traditional library information retrieval systems are:

- Poorly designed;
- Too time-consuming;
- Too difficult to use; and
- Unlikely to meet the information requirements of the customer.

Before we assume that the fault lies with the customer, we need to reevaluate our information systems and services and see how well or poorly they perform from the customer's perspective. To do this, we first look at the general characteristics of library information retrieval systems and then at the ways in which researchers —the most sophisticated library clients—use the library. By looking at our information systems from the customer's viewpoint, we may learn why so many of our potential customers avoid using the library.

SCHOLARLY DISCONTENT

> Competence, like truth, beauty, and contact lenses, is in the eye of the beholder.
> —Laurence Peter and Raymond Hull

If any group could be expected to be effective users of the library, it would be faculty and graduate students. Certainly it would be difficult to identify any other group that would be more literate, intelligent, and sophisticated users of the library and research materials. In almost every respect, scholars should be both the most appreciative and warmest supporter of libraries. Unfortunately, as Rebecca Watson-Boone's (1994, p. 213) brilliant analysis of recent studies of the information-seeking behavior of humanities scholars found, even humanities scholars use libraries as a last resort. Watson-Boone concludes that it now appears that scholars are not ignorant of, nor are they blindly indifferent to, library services, but, rather, they appear to be making a conscious choice *not* to use libraries in the way librarians think they should—"humanists will not use what they do not need."

Other distinguished librarians have recently uttered equally heretical critiques of librarians and the institutions they have constructed. For example, Patricia Battin (1986, p. 256), in an often discussed paper, notes that the evidence indicates that libraries have been storehouses where librarians "mark and park" rather than user-centered information sources central to the education and research function of the university. Joan Bechtel (1986, pp. 219–220) comes to the same conclusion when she notes that academic libraries have too often been seen as "warehouses for the storage of books" rather than as "centers of intellectual activity"; and Ross Atkinson (1993, pp. 458–460) waded in with a thoughtful piece that acknowledges the estrangement of academic libraries from the intellectual life of the university.

One of the most caustic attacks on library practices was delivered by Umberto Eco, who (in the wake of the publication of his enormously successful novel *The Name of the Rose*) was invited to address an audience of librarians in Milan, Italy. Eco stunned his audience by venting decades of frustration at the user-hostile nature of the libraries of the world. His strongest invective was reserved for the fact that: "librarians and not actual library users" determine the organization of library holdings, thus rendering the collections inaccessible to the experts who produce the contents of libraries and represent the natural users of libraries. He concluded, in a speech that no one seems interested in translating into English, that librarians have created an "immense nightmare" for users and that librarians are engaged in a "conservative, misconceived, even pathetic, last-ditch, attempt to salvage the 'status quo'" (quoted in Garrett, 1991, p. 385). Dan Hazen (1995, p. 30) recognizes the gravity of this problem and challenges librarians to acknowledge that they have become so oblivious to the needs of users that our access systems are "exercises in obsolescence and cater to nostalgic longings for order, precision and prescription."

SOME LIMITATIONS OF CURRENT INFORMATION
RETRIEVAL SYSTEMS

The libraries of today are warehouses for passive objects. The books and journals
sit on the shelves, waiting for us to use our intelligence to find them, read them,
interpret them, and finally make them divulge their stored knowledge. 'Electronic'
libraries of today are not better. Their pages are pages of data files, but the

electronic page images are equally passive.
—Edward Feigenbaum, Pamela McCorduck, and H. Penny Nii,
The Rise of the Expert Company

The recognition that contemporary information retrieval systems are not meeting user needs is not a recent development. Van Rijsbergen (1979, p. 5), for example, notes:

> Since the 1940s the problem of information storage and retrieval has attracted increasing attention. It is simply stated: we have vast amounts of information to which accurate and speedy access is becoming ever more difficult. One effect of this is that relevant information gets ignored since it is never uncovered, which in turn leads to much duplication of work and effort.

With few exceptions, most of the problems associated with information retrieval systems are attributed to the enormous and growing size of the research literature. Terms such as "infoglut" and "information overload," for instance, highlight the concern of information scientists with the sheer difficulty and complexity of storing and accessing today's databases. Despite the rapid advances in computer technology, few would argue with Lancaster (1991, p. 8) that "while technological advances have undoubtedly increased physical access to sources of information, it is very doubtful that intellectual access has improved significantly, if at all." It seems that the advances in computer hardware have, at best, sufficed to compensate for the growth in the literature. For the potential client, our current information retrieval systems excel only in delivering a large number of bibliographic citations of unknown quality.

Two decades ago librarians could take comfort in knowing that although their information systems were far from perfect, technological constraints limited them to re-creating computerized equivalents of their manual systems. In the age of the Internet, our customers have come to expect systems that provide functionality that goes beyond the card catalog's author, title, subject access. Most alarming of all, our customers now expect computer systems to be easy to use (graphical interfaces), convenient (full text), and powerful (multimedia, advanced search features, and customized for each user). It is becoming painfully clear that simply continuing to provide the traditional retrieval functions in the same old ways will no longer meet the expectations or needs of our customers.

RETRIEVING IDEAS—NOT CITATIONS

It is possible to store the mind with a million facts and still be entirely uneducated.
—Alec Bourne

Unfortunately, the rapid growth in the volume of literature that must be stored and retrieved is not the only problem confronting users of information retrieval systems. There is a growing awareness that contemporary information retrieval systems "are primitive and prevent the full utilization of this information" (Parsaye et al., 1989, p. 25). The traditional information retrieval system "does not inform (i.e., change the knowledge of) the user on the subject of his inquiry. It merely informs him on the existence (or nonexistence) and whereabouts of documents relating to his request" (Lancaster, 1968, p. 5). In other words, current information retrieval systems are misnamed. They do not retrieve information; rather, they retrieve bibliographic citations. The bibliographic citations, of course, do not reflect the rich network of interrelationships that exist in any scientific discipline. In fact, the resulting list of citations is so devoid of structure that it is usually arranged by the author's last name.

Researchers see their discipline in terms of information that is organized by theoretical concepts. To meet their informational needs, they want a source that shares an understanding of the major topics and paradigms in their field. What they emphatically do not want is a voluminous bibliography. As we have seen, reported research has consistently revealed that 1) libraries are a minor source of information for scholars and researchers, and 2) the most frequently consulted sources are colleagues, personal book and journal collections, and the collections of colleagues (Dougherty, 1990, p. 60). The same studies have also revealed that researchers and scholars often feel that "librarians organize libraries to serve the needs of librarians rather than those of users" (p. 60). Librarians and information scientists have usually discredited the preceding criticisms by noting that most researchers are not skilled library users. While this is a convenient and comfortable explanation, it overlooks one salient fact: "Users seek information from those sources they find most productive, convenient, and timely. This explains why personal collections and colleagues are so frequently consulted" (p. 62).

Rather than assert that researchers do not know how to use information sources, it might be more accurate to note that researchers do not use information sources in the same way that librarians do. While information scientists might begin their study by consulting the appropriate indexes, searching the card catalog, and conducting an exhaustive online search, researchers prefer to consult colleagues and browse through relevant documents. According to Parsaye et al. (1989, p. 282), the major advantage of browsing is that researchers not only get to see the information in the document immediately, but, more important, once they have tracked down a concept in one document, that document's footnotes can then be used to guide the researchers to related concepts in other documents. The ability to trace related concepts through references allows researchers to view their literature as a complex structure that is held together by the main paradigms of the field. In sharp contrast, the linking mechanism used in a conventional information retrieval system is limited to some type of Boolean search that, of necessity, ignores the interconnections that exist among documents.

Instead of cavalierly dismissing the alleged failure of researchers to use the contemporary information retrieval tools as evidence that they do not know how to use a library, the profession would be better advised to reexamine the serious limitations of current information retrieval systems. When the first online information retrieval systems appeared in the 1960s, it seemed that electronic access might be the answer to accessing the rapidly growing databases. In fact, Parsaye et al. (1989, p. 7) argue that in many cases the electronic availability of information may serve more as a distracter, preventing one from finding what is really relevant, much as a needle gets lost in a haystack." The challenge for librarians today is clear. The pressing need is to develop a new paradigm for organizing information that will allow researchers to retrieve ideas—not bibliographic citations.

LIBRARY ACCESS TOOLS

> There it was, hidden in alphabetical order.
> —Rita Holt

With few exceptions, users do not use the elaborate and sophisticated finding tools that have for centuries been the pride of the library profession. They may, according to Mann (1993, p. 75), use the classification scheme for browsing, but they nearly always ignore the subject headings and journal indexes. They rely, almost exclusively, on browsing in the stacks, talking to colleagues, and footnote chasing (p. 88).

As might be expected, librarians have long deplored such behavior. After all, the library's finding tools represent the culmination of centuries of work and thought. For many librarians the traditional library access tools—classification, subject headings, precoordinate indexing, and the catalog—represent the noblest and greatest achievements of the profession. Their pride in this great achievement is certainly understandable because they created the most advanced paper-based retrieval system in history. Even before the advent of the computer, librarians had nearly achieved the ultimate goal of the traditional library vision: universal bibliographic control. Most impressive of all, they managed to create this magnificent system using only their intelligence, typewriters, and 3 × 5 cards.

Of course, the magnitude of the task and the limitations of paper-based information retrieval systems made the system extremely complex to use. Even something seemingly as simple as filing rules for the catalog turns out, in practice, to be amazingly complex. Many librarians, not to mention the hapless customer, remain blissfully ignorant of the many arcane rules that determine if the entry for Louis XIV precedes or follows Louis IX. In fact, the filing rules are so complex that entire books have been written on the subject. Clearly, such a system, despite its brilliant achievements, was never designed for ease of use. It was (and remains) an enormously complicated inventory tool that allowed librarians to record the location of each edition of every monograph owned by the library. Since the first priority was to maintain an accurate record of the library's collection, our bibliographic records naturally were optimized for inventory control, not access. As a result, it is relatively easy to determine the size of the book (in centimeters, of course), the edition, or the number of pages in the bibliography. In sharp contrast to the wealth of details about the physical characteristics provided about each volume in the collection, information concerning the subject content of the monograph is, by today's standards, woefully inadequate.

Although library customers do find that classifying and shelving books by subject area is useful for browsing, grouping titles by subject provides a very limited subject access. Since there can be only one physical ordering on the shelves, there is no way to represent the interdisciplinary content of a book or show its relationship to other subject areas. Another limitation of the library's classification scheme is that it cannot provide access to serials. The problem is that the subject content of journal articles is too complicated to be adequately described by a classification scheme for one obvious reason: A "long run of bound volumes of the journal may contain articles on thousands of subjects (often dozens within a single issue)" (Mann, 1993, p. 23).

At the beginning of the 20th century, cataloging and the card catalog represented the most sophisticated paper-based access system in existence. The card catalog in particular offered multiple access points, random access, and virtually unlimited expandability. Librarians have every right to be proud of their marvelous creation. At the dawn of the 21st century, however, there are unmistakable signs that the card catalog and its close relative, the OPAC, are both as obsolete as the electric typewriter. Admittedly, the OPAC still does a creditable job of providing a marvelous inventory of the library's holdings, but the library's clients have no interest in using a sophisticated inventory tool. What they want and what they expect is an information retrieval system that offers the same kind of quick, painless access to the collection that is offered by Web searchers such as Yahoo; Alta Vista, Lycos, and Expert Search.

Unfortunately, what they get—even from the best OPACs—is a very clumsy user interface that provides only rudimentary subject access to the collection. It is an interface that one software designer scathingly described in the following terms (Zimmermann, 1993, p. 57):

> The user interface for conventional Boolean proximity search is terrible. It does not provide enough feedback to let the user avoid subtle (or obvious) mistakes, it requires too much human memory and creative energy in query formulation, and it gets in the way of seeing the data. Often, an apparently innocuous term deep inside a parenthesized Boolean search statement actually distorts the entire meaning of the query and eliminates all the useful information that was to be retrieved.

As a result of its serious limitations, even the most expensive and elaborate OPAC adds little value for the library's customers. Studies have repeatedly found that between 35 and 50 percent of all subject searches carried out by library patrons retrieve no hits (Markey, 1986, p. 60). More than "50 percent of the people using the catalog will look up only one entry and stop, regardless of whether or not they have found what they are looking for" (Mann, 1993, p. 100). With such an abysmal success rate, it is little wonder that the library's clientele strenuously avoids using the OPAC. It is also difficult to justify the cost of maintaining a retrieval system that routinely fails half the time—especially when the cost of cataloging a book is now more than $75 per volume (Mann, 1993, p. 20).

Despite years of bibliographic instruction and mandatory classes on using the library, user studies routinely find that the library's complex access tools do not meet the needs of the library's clientele. Mann (1993, p. 167) suggests that the problem might be ameliorated if every bibliographic instruction class emphasized the necessity of asking the librarians for help. Mann (pp. 167–168) then notes out that "even graduate students need help from the professional librarian."

Quite unintentionally, Mann has pointed out that because of their complexity and design flaws, the library's access tools are virtually useless to the overwhelming majority of the public. Since our access tools are unusable, the obvious solution is to develop new access tools. Of course, such a development would mean that we would have to give client convenience a higher priority than collection maintenance (inventory control). Again, if the library community were genuinely committed to adding value for its customers, there is no doubt that libraries would have begun a major reengineering effort to jettison their antiquated and collection-centered access tools and replace them with new software that is designed for ease of use. To put these criticisms in perspective, just imagine how much business America On Line would do if every customer required several hours of onsite instruction and then, after the classes, still had to call a technician every time he or she wanted to search the Internet. To insist that libraries should continue to spend their meager resources building access tools that are not usable by the general public is simply suicidal.

Although there is overwhelming evidence that the current set of access tools fails to meet customer needs, there remains a powerful majority of library professionals who agree with Mann (1993, p. 189) that "it is a mistake for librarians to believe that the work of cataloging can be abandoned in the expectation of the imminent arrival of expert-system or artificial intelligence programs. . . ." When we see many of our brightest professionals continue to defend an access system that was not designed to meet user needs and has a decades-old record of failure, we can see just how powerful the traditional library vision remains. Thus, Mann (p. 189) can write that "it is a mistake to think that the mere acquisition of books without proper cataloging renders them accessible . . . " without ever pausing to remember that information-seeking studies have invariably found that the library's customers have not, do not, and will not use the current library access tools.

LIBRARY OF CONGRESS SUBJECT HEADINGS

> The information we have is not what we want. The information we want is not
> what we need. The information we need is not available.
> —John Peers, *1,001 Logical Laws*

The Library of Congress Subject Headings (LCSH) were designed to provide limited subject access to the monograph collection. At the time of their development, they represented a most ingenious solution to a very serious problem. The crux of the problem was how to provide subject access to thousands of books while limiting the number of subject entry terms. The number of subject entry terms had to be strictly limited. Without such a limitation, the card catalog would quickly become prohibitively expensive. The solution was to create a limited set of approved subject headings, assigned to each monograph when it was cataloged. This procedure provided rudimentary subject access at a practical cost.

On average, about 2.5 subject headings are assigned per title. Obviously, this limited number of subject headings cannot provide in-depth or exhaustive indexing. To make matters even worse, the subject headings are precoordinated, which means that the searcher cannot combine subject terms at the time of the search. Thus, if a person wants to retrieve books on the U.S. Civil War, the researcher cannot simply enter the search terms: U.S., Civil and War. Instead the researcher must use the approved subject heading that has been assigned to the book as part of the cataloging process. In this example, the searcher is required to type in the following search: History-United States-Civil War, 1861–1865. If the researcher wants to locate books about a specific battle, such as, Nashville, then once again the client has to enter the approved subject heading (in this case: **). Of course, the researcher cannot combine or arrange the terms to match more precisely his or her subject material. In fact, as Gregor and Mandel (1991, p. 47) note, online subject-searching studies have shown that users rarely enter subject terms exactly—they are especially frustrated by long strings; and users do not use subject terms precisely—fine distinctions are meaningless to them and may, in fact, mislead them. As might be expected, once keyword searching became available, precoordinated subject headings lost what little appeal they had ever possessed.

Despite their total irrelevance to customer needs, librarians continue to invest time and effort in assigning precoordinated subject headings. Mann (1993, p. 42) notes that "it is truly unusual to find any readers who can locate on their own the proper subject heading(s) for their topic." In fact, he continues, "it is not uncommon for graduate students to go through their program without ever knowing about the existence of the LCSH list." Not surprisingly, the library's customers have already figured out that neither the card catalog nor its offspring, the OPAC, provides a useful subject access tool. Peters (1991, p. 96) notes that "approximately 80 percent of all subject searches bypass the subject catalog."

In a 1991 study, Lancaster (p. 5) searched 51 topics on an OPAC and then compared the results of the searches with reading lists on the topics prepared by subject experts. He found that ". . . the online searches retrieve relatively few of the best items even when broadened so much that several hundred items are retrieved in a search." Lancaster (p. 6) concludes that:

> [I]t appears that very little could be done to make these items more retrievable. A more sophisticated Boolean search capability is not the solution since it is rare that more than one facet of a search topic is represented anywhere in a record: subject headings, classification numbers, or keywords in titles. The bibliographic records are just too brief to allow effective subject searches. Storing contents pages or book indexes could raise recall in the 51 searches from about 59% to around 90% but at a great cost, and would retrieve thousands of items per search rather than hundreds. A very detailed level of analytical subject cataloging could greatly improve the situation, but this solution would also be very costly. Moreover, it would not provide the complete solution because the relevance of certain items to various topics is unlikely to be seen by any but the subject specialist.

According to Lancaster (1991, p. 6), "library catalogs permit only the most superficial of subject searches." Their utility is further lessened because they rarely include periodical articles, continues Lancaster (p. 6), and they provide access only at the level of the complete bibliographic item rather than at the level of a chapter, article, conference paper, or paragraph. In other words, the library catalog, in its current form, "is quite inadequate for a large multidisciplinary library, especially one that attempts to support educational or scholarly needs." The situation would not be improved by providing sophisticated searching software because the bibliographic records stored in the catalog "are completely inadequate representations of the subject matter dealt with" (p. 6). Lancaster's (pp. 6–7) concluding remarks make it clear that all of the students who ignored their bibliographic instruction and all of those researchers who ignored library searching guidelines might have been right after all:

> [T]he results suggest that significant improvements are not possible within the constraints of existing subject cataloging practice. The conclusion [that] emerges most clearly is that, if one wants to know the best things to read on some topic, there is no substitute for consulting an expert, either directly or indirectly (e.g., through an expert-compiled bibliography).
>
> This conclusion should not come as much of a surprise. Investigations over many years have consistently shown that seekers of information find much of what they use from specialized bibliographies or bibliographic references in items already known, rather than from databases, library catalogs or consulting librarians.

Of course, Lancaster's viewpoint is not endorsed by all librarians, perhaps not even by a majority. Mann (1993, p. 143), the brilliant defender of the status quo, argues fervently that substituting keyword access in place of the LCSH would seriously damage the retrieval capabilities of a research library. Certainly Mann, like so many librarians, would violently disagree with Peters's (1991, pp. 233–234) speculation about the future of the catalog:

> The crisis of the concept of a library catalog, wrought by technological advances may lead to the complete obsolescence of the library catalog. The demands and expectations of users, as their needs and interests slowly move away from information normally contained in a library catalog, require a new means of providing bibliographic control.

DO LIBRARIES NEED A NEW VISION? WARNING SIGNS

> Vision always deals with the future. Indeed, vision is where tomorrow begins, for it expresses what you and others who share the vision will be working hard to create. Since most people don't take the time to think systematically about the future, those who do—and who base their strategies and actions on their visions— have inordinate power to shape the future.
> —Burt Nanus (1992)

Over the past decade, advances in computer technology, graphical interfaces, the Internet, and software design have caused thoughtful librarians to reexamine their professional values. What kind of vision do we need to inspire the next generation of librarians so that they can deal with a world in which the very idea of library has been transmuted? Although we do not know precisely what the new library will look like, there are clues to what some of its main features will be. For instance, a *New York Times* article envisioned the library as follows:

> [T]omorrow's library will not necessarily be a place to go . . . but rather a focal point for a variety of services. Such "libraries without wall[s]" are beginning to appear in schools and businesses, and the silent, musty stacks are giving way to high-technology centers, available to personal computers everywhere. (Lewis, 1990, p. 8f)

K.H. Bacon, an official of the Library of Congress, told a *Wall Street Journal* reporter that the "libraries of the future will be a service, not a place" (1990, p. B3). Clearly it is time for reflective librarians to rethink the purpose, role, and future of their institution. In *Visionary Leadership*, Nanus (1992, pp. 19–20) lists some of the warning signs that indicate that an established vision is becoming obsolete. As we read through this list, we need to ask ourselves how many of these questions are true of our libraries:

1. Is there evidence of confusion about purpose? Are there disagreements among key staff members about which customers or clients should have priority or which services and technologies are the most important?
2. Do the employees complain about a lack of challenge or boredom?
3. Is the organization losing legitimacy, its clientele, or reputation for innovation?
4. Do outsiders sometimes suggest that your organization may be slipping or not keeping up with changes in technology?
5. Do people shelter behind their narrow job descriptions and avoid risk by refusing to accept responsibility or ownership for new projects?
6. Is there an absence of shared accomplishments?
7. Is there an overactive rumor mill? Do people try to find out through the grapevine what is in store for them?

We believe that, if answered candidly, most librarians would have to concede that libraries no longer have a clear vision of their social role, that our libraries are not keeping up with technology, that many library employees shelter behind their bureaucratic job descriptions, and that our libraries have not developed any innovative programs in years.

The same technology that has threatened to make so many of our programs and practices obsolete also offers us the opportunity to provide a new level of service for our clients that will, in effect, transform the library from a warehouse into a customized provider of information.

The challenge for information scientists is clear. The pressing need is to develop a new paradigm for organizing information that will allow the library to become more than a warehouse of printed material.

7

Toward the Information Future: Libraries as Knowledge Bases

By adding "intelligence" to information processing and management, otherwise daunting tasks (such as retrieving relevant information from a vast database) can be greatly simplified.
—*Cyberspace Lexicon*

INFORMATION OVERLOAD AND THE LIBRARY

Everybody gets so much information all day long that they lose their common sense.
—Gertrude Stein, *Reflections on the Atomic Bomb*

The need to develop new tools for accessing, storing, and manipulating data becomes more pressing every year. To survive in today's society requires access to large amounts of the most accurate and current data available. Without access to large amounts of quality information, we simply have no way of objectively analyzing our problems, for we have built a "civilization so complex" that improved information access is essential to the decision-making process in both our personal lives and our work (Bush, 1945, p. 108).

By the end of the 19th century, information overload was already a serious problem (Parsaye et al., 1989, p. 156). During the 20th century, ". , . our ability to accumulate information has increased exponentially over time" (Parsaye & Chignell, 1993, p. 5). Unfortunately, our ability to make effective use of the vast amounts of information available to us in the world's databases has not kept pace with our ability to store data. Paradoxically, the development of computers and information systems has been tantamount to pouring gasoline on a raging fire (p. 6).

Despite—or in many cases because of—our computerized information systems, we are increasingly drowning in the glut of information. Instead of providing quality information, tailored to the needs of the customer, our systems overwhelm us with raw data, giving a profound meaning to T. S. Eliot's lament: "Where is the wisdom we have lost in knowledge? Where is the knowledge we have lost in information?" (1963, p. 147)

To paraphrase Eliot, it is little wonder that information-system users are wondering where the information is that they have lost in their voluminous printouts or multiple screen displays. Online systems are attractive for many individuals because full-text systems combine the querying and the delivery subsystems; that is, once a desired item has been found, it is instantly available to the user. At the same time, online systems are frustrating ". . . because our methods of retrieving all this information are primitive and prevent the full utilization of this information" (Parsaye et al., 1989, p. 25).

This unhappy state of affairs is not limited to business or academia. Anyone using an OPAC in a large research library can attest that finding the right book requires persistence and considerable luck. The magnitude of the problem facing the library user is captured by Parsaye and Chignell (1993, pp. 7, 9) in the following passage:

> Consider a book like *War and Peace* or the *Bible*. How long would it take you to read either? Now imagine the millions of books that have been published. How many of them contain useful ideas or information that you will never read? It is one thing to be selective, but quite another to be ignorant. We never get the chance to see how much of this excess information might actually be useful to us.
>
> As books multiplied after the invention of movable type, up-to-date and useful information about various topics became dispersed amongst books from different sources and authorities. As the quantity of information increased, the quality began to suffer and it became more difficult to "find the right book."

A more concrete example of how online library systems complicate access for our customers is illustrated by the technically sophisticated online retrieval system of the University of California. This immense system accesses the catalogs of all the libraries in the California system from anywhere in the world. Ostensibly the system provides instant access to millions of items, but a recent study found that 40 percent of all user subject searches returned zero hits and the other 60 percent of user queries returned an average of 700 hits (Landauer, 1995, p. 253). About the kindest thing that can be said about this system is that it is no worse than most large OPACs.

Because our traditional methods of storing, indexing, and accessing data cannot organize and describe the enormous volume of data that is being generated by our so-called information systems, we need some tool that will allow us to separate "the informational wheat from the surrounding chaff" (Parsaye et al., 1989, p. 7). What is needed is a new kind of database that will allow us "to make full use of the vast information resources that are now available and that are being added to daily." Although still in their formative stages, intelligent databases have the capability of retrieving, displaying, disseminating and combining text and multimedia information in totally new ways (p. 25).

Intelligent databases, unlike contemporary search engines, would take over the task of determining how to perform the search. Searchers would only be required to state what information they wanted, not to specify how to extract the required information. The great advantage of this approach is that users no longer would have to worry about supervising the search process; instead they could concentrate on the more important task of evaluating the results of their search.

LIMITATIONS OF THE TRADITIONAL INDEXING PARADIGM

> Thus far we seem to be worse off than before—for we can enormously extend the record; yet even in its present bulk we can hardly consult it. This is a much larger matter than merely the extraction of data for the purposes of scientific research; it involves the entire process by which man profits by his inheritance of acquired knowledge. The prime action of use is selection, and here we are halting indeed. The real heart of the matter of selection, however, goes deeper than a lag in the adoption of mechanisms by libraries, or a lack of development of devices for their use. Our ineptitude in getting at the record is largely caused by the artificiality of systems of indexing.
> —Vannevar Bush (1945)

The goal of information retrieval systems is to retrieve all the relevant documents and at the same time retrieve as few of the nonrelevant as possible. Traditional retrieval systems such as library OPACs, online databases, relational databases, and most Internet search engines base their retrieval strategies on a simple matching process. The user enters subject terms, which are then matched against the indexing terms stored in the database. Conceptually, the index terms act as a surrogate for each of the documents that have been indexed. The system will work marvelously if searcher and indexer use the same identifiers to describe a particular concept. Unfortunately, the richness of natural languages and the variability of humans make it unlikely that the searcher and the indexer will agree on a "best" term. In fact, studies have repeatedly shown that even when authors provide multiple index terms, retrieval accuracy based on word matching fails more often than it succeeds (Landauer et al., 1993, p. 76).

The fundamental nature of the indexing problem is illustrated by a story recounted by Parsaye et al. (1989, p. 297). The researchers visited a major database producer. As part of their research, they asked professional indexers to assign index terms based on abstracts from one of the company's databases. The researchers found that

> no two indexers could agree on a set of index terms for any of the documents and spirited discussions (arguments) quickly broke out among the indexers. These discussions arose because the indexers could not agree on the meaning of the text, could not agree on the way that index terms should be assigned to a particular concept represented in the text, or some combination of these two disagreements.

Based on the studies carried out by Furnas and his associates (1983 and 1987), one solution to the indexing problem appears to be to list every term used by people to describe the document and then index by all of these terms. This indexing technique, which is called either "unlimited aliasing" or "rich indexing," performed well. Simulations showed that "rich indexing" improved recall by a factor of 4—from about 20 percent to nearly 80 percent with minimal adverse effects on precision (Landauer et al.,1993, p. 76).

Of course, such an approach would be completely impractical in the paper-and-ink world of the card catalog because the prospect of 30 catalog cards for every book or 30 index entries for every chapter would be prohibitively expensive. In moderate-size databases, the approach works well, according to Landauer et al. (1993, p. 77). In large databases, however, this type of indexing would encounter the same low-precision problems that plague full-text indexing.

One standard, albeit largely unsuccessful, solution for improving the precision of a retrieval system is to allow users to combine words and phrases using Boolean expressions. Although Boolean logic provides a powerful and universal method of narrowing searches, it suffers from two inherent and major problems. First, most people find it extremely difficult to construct logically correct expressions or sentences (see Borgman, 1986; Greene, Gomez, & Devlin, 1986, pp. 9–13; and Greene, Cannata, & Gomez, 1990, p. 303). Parsaye et al. (1989, p. 308; see also Johnson-Laird, 1988, and Landauer, 1995), note that the evidence clearly indicates that the formation and comprehension of logical expressions exceed "normal human information processing limitations for the population at large." Since our query languages do not reflect "the way ordinary people think or by the way people ordinarily use words," a majority of the library users find "Boolean-speak" to be so difficult and, in practice, so unreliable that they simply avoid using conventional information retrieval systems (Landauer, 1995, p. 147).

The second problem with Boolean operators is that the probability of the searcher selecting two terms that exactly match the same two words used by an indexer to describe a document is so low that recall is drastically lowered anytime searchers use Boolean ANDs in their search statements. Since studies have shown that, on average, a searcher has a 1 in 6 chance of guessing the word that another person has selected as the index term, the odds of correctly guessing two different terms gets dramatically worse: 1 in 36 (Landauer et al., 1993, pp. 77–78). This simple example underscores why the AND operator is far more likely to eliminate relevant documents than it is to ignore irrelevant material (Landauer, 1995, p. 261).

In his delightful book *Things That Make Us Smart*, Donald A. Norman observes that people do not operate by mathematical or symbolic logic. In fact, the reason we invented symbolic logic was to supplement our limited ability to analyze abstract problems. Because "logic is most definitely not a good model of human cognition," it makes no sense to require searchers to know and understand Boolean logic (Norman, 1993, p. 228).

Landauer (1995, p. 260) recounts an anecdote that illustrates the problems that most people have when attempting to use Boolean operators: "A story famous among reference librarians tells of a user who asked the online system for titles containing Navajo AND Indian. Getting no hits, the user then asked for Navajo AND Indian AND Arizona."

Even under ideal conditions—subject experts searching specialized databases—traditional text retrieval systems perform poorly. In a 1985 case study of a legal search system, Blair and Maron (1985, pp. 280–281) asked professional searchers to search a legal database until they were sure that they had retrieved at least 70 percent of the relevant material stored in the database. When the researchers carried out an exhaustive search of the database, they found that the professional searchers had located less than 20 percent of the relevant documents.

Landauer and colleagues (1993, p. 75) summarizes the current failings of conventional retrieval systems in the following passage:

> Extensive empirical data on the success of searchers finding relevant documents (actually, usually abstracts of longer documents) in small to very large collections is both consistent and depressing. There is always a direct relation between finding lots of things that are wanted and getting lots of things that are not. Finding half of the documents in a collection that are really relevant while collecting only half "junk" is about the best that can be expected from state-of-the-art methods.

Landauer concludes by observing that in study after study, searchers using traditional information retrieval systems typically find from 10 to 40 percent of the relevant materials while getting 30 to 60 percent unwanted materials. Surprisingly, the recall and precision percentages for both the most advanced computer-based retrieval systems and paper-based systems seem to be about the same (see Cleverdon, 1984; Salton & McGill, 1983; and Van Rijsbergen, 1979). As long as the traditional indexing paradigm is used, advanced computer technology can speed up the searching process, but it cannot make a qualitative improvement in the retrieval process.

PROBLEMS WITH CLASSICAL ACCESS METHODS: HIERARCHIES

> I wish people who have trouble communicating would just shut up.
> —Tom Lehrer

Just as there are cogent reasons to develop knowledge-based information retrieval systems that do not rely on Boolean operators, there are also persuasive reasons for developing systems that do not rely on monolithic hierarchical organizational schemes. Norman (1993, p. 178) identifies three major problems with hierarchical classification schemes. First, as catalogers can attest, there is no scheme that can categorize documents into one and only one position in the hierarchy. In most cases subject terms frequently cross disciplines, which makes it impossible to assign them to a unique location. In addition, where we expect to find a term depends in part upon what use we intend to make of it (see Winograd & Flores, 1986, on the importance of context for meaning).

The second problem is that our categories change over time. We need only look at the subject headings used by catalogers to classify monographs on computer languages to realize how quickly classification schemes can become obsolete in rapidly changing fields (Norman, 1993, p. 178).

The third problem is that complex organizational structures are difficult to navigate. Unless the searcher is extremely familiar with the categories, the very complexity of the scheme can cause the searcher to become lost in the maze of subdivisions. When we combine minutely detailed classification schemes, traditional indexing, and Boolean operators in our traditional retrieval systems, we create systems that are so complex that only a quarter of the students at Stanford could use the library's online catalog after several hours of instruction (Borgman, 1986). To add to our embarrassment, our most sophisticated retrieval systems, running on the most powerful computers available, "routinely fail to break the 50/50 limit— find half of the relevant documents in the database and half of what is retrieved is relevant" (Landauer, 1995, p. 261). It is painfully obvious that we need to devise new retrieval tools that match our human capabilities. In fact, we need to transform our current information retrieval systems into intelligent databases.

THE PROMISE OF INTELLIGENT KNOWLEDGE-BASES

> There is a growing mountain of research. But there is increased evidence that we are being bogged down today as specialization extends. The investigator is staggered by the findings and conclusions of thousands of other workers—

conclusions which he cannot find time to grasp,
much less to remember as they appear.
—Vannevar Bush (1945)

Conceptually, the next step is obvious: Develop intelligent knowledge-bases that will store not only facts about individual documents but also the linkages that exist among the documents. These hypertext databases would provide the user with an abstract model of the subject specialty that would closely resemble the researcher's working model. In a very real sense, such a database could be correctly termed a "knowledge-base." Although an intelligent knowledge-base would, like Parsaye et al.'s (1989, p. 18) intelligent database, "manage information in a natural way, making that information easy to store, access, and use," intelligent knowledge-bases would also provide hypertext links to literature reviews, historical overviews, and selected bibliographies for each discipline or research topic. Such databases would equip information scientists with a retrieval tool that would at last equal the power of Vannevar Bush's famed Memex. The Memex (memory extender) is Bush's (1945, p. 107) name for the individualized, private file organizer and personal library that would act as "an enlarged intimate supplement" to the researcher's memory. Most important, Memex would, like the human mind, be able to retrieve information by associating ideas—not by matching index terms (Bush, 1945, p. 106; see also Reichgelt, 1991).

Unlike Bush's Memex, intelligent knowledge-bases are not imaginary artifacts— nor, for that matter, science fiction. They are quite real and the outgrowth of the confluence of two key technologies. The first is the traditional online retrieval system, with its processing and mass storage capabilities. The second utilizes two features of the Internet: the hypermedia searching capability of HTML and the power of specialized Web agents that have the intelligence to constantly search large databases for the precise information that an individual has requested. Such specialized agents, called spiders, can search through the contents of every document, journal article, or Web site stored on either the Internet or an intranet and then automatically notify the user when relevant documents are located (Cheong, 1996, pp. 82–83). By combining the power of associative databases with ease of use of the Internet, we now have the capability of constructing online retrieval systems that can represent documents in terms of concepts rather than keywords; in short, the technological tools needed to build databases that can truly represent the intellectual framework of a discipline are now available.

The design of the complex knowledge representation schemes needed to construct intelligent databases will be a difficult and costly task. However, the availability of sophisticated software packages such as FrontPage or Netscape Communicator have greatly simplified the construction and maintenance of Web sites. Using such powerful Web builders frees the builders of intelligent knowledge-bases from the need to encode every line in HTML, thereby allowing subject specialists to concentrate on the most difficult and most valuable part of any knowledge-base: content (Bradley & Nolan, 1998, p. 79).

DEVELOPING INTELLIGENT KNOWLEDGE-BASES: COSTS

> Make no small plans . . . for they have not the power to stir men's blood.
> —Niccolo Machiavelli, *The Prince*

Like so many other software innovations, intelligent knowledge-bases have not been immune to overselling and hyperbole. Undoubtedly, the development of Internet-based knowledge-bases will require a major investment in time, talent, and effort. Because the developers of knowledge-bases must have an in-depth knowledge of the literature, research issues, and contending paradigms of the subject area, the personnel costs associated with the development of knowledge-bases will be high.

Another major development cost, and one likely to be overlooked by library administrators, is the cost of experimenting with the new technology. As Senge notes, "significant innovation cannot be achieved by talking about new ideas; you must build and test prototypes" (1990, p. 271). Only by actually constructing, testing, and then modifying the initial models of the intelligent knowledge-bases will we be able to solve the problems that stand between the initial idea of knowledge-based information systems and its full and successful implementation.

CHARACTERISTICS OF AN INTELLIGENT KNOWLEDGE-BASE

> It is a very sad thing that nowadays there is so little useless information.
> —Oscar Wilde

Despite their costs, the development of intelligent databases offers libraries the opportunity to provide new levels of service. For the first time, libraries have the capability to provide expert guidance to every customer. Intelligent databases also offer libraries a means of replacing their outmoded information retrieval systems— systems that Bush (1945, p. 101) described half a century ago as being "totally inadequate" for "transmitting and reviewing the results of research."

At a minimum, intelligent databases will:

- Be easy to use;
- Handle large amounts of information;
- Manipulate many different types of media (text, graphics, audio, pictures, and animation);
- Improve decision making by extracting knowledge from data by using high-level information models;
- Require minimal instruction;
- Target individual information needs;

- Provide personalized service;
- Offer different levels of detail for each patron;
- Provide context-sensitive help that will explain the structure of the discipline; and
- Reflect the relationships and internal structure of the discipline.

As is apparent from this list of attributes, intelligent databases are simply the latest in a long line of tools that we have used to enhance our cognitive abilities. Norman (1993, p. 3) argues most persuasively that "the human mind is limited in capability." Norman continues:

> There is only so much we can remember, only so much we can learn. But among our abilities is that of devising artificial devices—artifacts—that expand our capabilities. We invent things that make us smart. Through technology, we can think better and more clearly. We have access to accurate information.
>
> Writing, reading, art, music, logic, the invention of encyclopedias and textbooks are examples of tools we have developed to make us smarter.

LIBRARIES TO MAKE US SMARTER

> We're drowning in information and starving for knowledge.
> —Rutherford D. Rogers, Librarian, Yale University

A few years ago, Penniman (1992, p. 40) summarized the social challenge that libraries face in the digital age when he noted that our ancestors

> could process symbols at about 300 units per minute, and so do we. This limitation— our inability to speed up our own processing capacity is symbolic of our greatest challenge: to assure that all the information (now stored, processed, and transmitted as bits) can be delivered as knowledge that is of use to humans.

In Penniman's opinion (1992, p. 40), our ability to use technology to transcend the limitations on our ability to understand is sorely limited, "not because we lack technological know-how, but because we lack strategic know-how." As we have seen, the old techniques of subject headings, keyword indexing, and hierarchical classification are difficult to use and perform poorly. What is needed is a database that is so automatic and so intuitive to use that we forget we are searching a database and instead focus exclusively on results of our search. In an intelligent database, the intellectual burden involved in composing queries is transferred from the searcher to the software. Unlike traditional information retrieval systems, which require searchers to modify their behavior to meet the needs of the retrieval system, an intelligent database is designed to accommodate itself to the meets the needs of each searcher (Norman, 1993, p. 180).

Although we have been describing intelligent databases as if there were only one type, there are already many variations on the model. In the following section we look at several of the models that seem to have the most promise. In most of the examples, however, we will see that the old matching paradigm is usually replaced by some type of "navigation by description" or "query by description." In query by description—or its cousin, query by example—the searcher does not need to formulate a complex Boolean argument that uses the preferred index terms. Instead, the searcher needs only to communicate a description of what kind of materials is wanted. A variation on the query by description technique is Parsaye's et al. (1989, p. 310) exploration model. In the exploratory paradigm (see also Belkin & Vickery, 1985), the searcher explores the information directly and picks out what seems appropriate.

Despite their differences in terminology, most of the new searching models that have been proposed for intelligent databases move closer to Vannevar Bush's dream of selection by association. Bush argues that the human mind does not work in a serial, logical fashion. The human mind "operates by association" (Bush, 1945, p. 106). The key point, in Bush's opinion, is that "associative indexing" would allow searchers to follow any path through a database that they desired. The heart of the database would no longer be isolated facts but ideas linked together in a rich network of associations. It is the linking together of ideas that is, for Bush (p. 107), "the important thing."

AN EXAMPLE OF A QUERY BY DESCRIPTION DATABASE

One of the great advantages of a database that uses navigation by description is that it allows searchers to learn while they search. Conventional retrieval systems demand that we pose a precise and specific query at the beginning of our search. Of course, when we are searching for information on a topic, we are seldom certain about either the question or the answer because the search process is fundamentally an exploration of a knowledge base. Because we learn during our navigation through the database, we will refine our initial concept of what we are looking for as we learn more about what is available.

In *Things that Make Us Smarter*, Norman (1993) describes an experimental database, designed by Michael Williams and Frederich Tou, that does not assume the searcher knows anything about the way the database stores its information or even that the searcher knows exactly what to ask.

The database, which Williams and Tou call Rabbit, contains information on 1,000 restaurants. In the traditional model, we would have to pose a precise query, such as "retrieve all restaurants that feature Chinese food, are inexpensive, and located on the west side of the city." Although the subject matter is different, this query is very similar to the kind of queries we routinely ask our customers to formulate when they try to find a book in the card catalog.

Rabbit's approach is much different because it is designed to help the searcher learn about the kinds of information the database needs. It accomplishes this task by selecting a restaurant. The searcher then uses the description of the restaurant as a starting point to indicate what features the searcher likes, dislikes, or is indifferent to by modifying any of the descriptive dimensions. Rabbit simplifies the process by providing a list of alternatives for each field. For example, let us assume that the first restaurant selected by Rabbit features American cuisine, is moderately priced, and is on the west side of town. The program lets the searcher highlight what features are desired. Rabbit then searches the database to retrieve restaurants that match those characteristics that the searcher has indicated are desirable. When the searcher begins to narrow the list of restaurants, he or she can request to see a list of restaurants similar to the one selected. Finally, the selection process can be modified by telling Rabbit not to retrieve any restaurants that share a particular attribute, such as having a cover charge.

The entire process is very natural. It emphasizes the powers of the human mind by letting the searcher do what comes naturally: that is, select from concrete examples rather than create an abstract description of the desired restaurant. In a sense, Rabbit is teaching the searcher how to use the database; however, it is carrying out the instructions on the searcher's terms, using the searcher's language. Although Rabbit never asks the searcher to enter a request using a logical statement, Rabbit is internally constructing queries that contain logical expressions that describe the searcher's likes and dislikes.

Although Rabbit was used only in the Xerox Palo Alto Research Center to study human–computer interactions, it nevertheless illustrates how computer technology can be used to give control to the searcher by using innovative software to translate the software's internal machine-centered logic into a representation that is easily understand by a person (Norman, 1993, p. 243). Many of the convenient features first used in Rabbit are now incorporated in Web search engines such as Yahoo!, Alta Vista, Lycos, or Expert. In particular, Expert now offers both convenience and a powerful search engine. Expert not only supports Query-by-Example, but its design allows the searcher to type in plain English queries. In fact, Expert's advanced search technology will perform better if the searcher types in a query such as "learn to speak Tagalog" rather than the standard Boolean search, which would require the searcher to enter: "Tagalog AND Learn." *Expert* also provides a list of the matching documents in decreasing order of confidence. The confidence rating provides a rough indicator to how closely the item matches the searcher's query. To further assist the searcher, the search result list also includes a brief summary of what the page is about. The summary is automatically generated by the proprietary search engine, Intelligent Concept Extraction.

INTERFACES AND CUSTOMER SATISFACTION

If such a computer [PC] is to be any more useful than a rock to the average person,
someone will have to write software that will communicate effectively.
This will not be easy. . . .
—Paul Heckel, *The Elements of Friendly Software Design*

While even the best of the Web search engines are far from perfect, they are much easier to use and provide much better subject access than an OPAC. Most of the current generation of Web search engines are programmed to allow the searcher to pose inexact queries, show partial matches, and ignore most spelling errors. Many of the search engines, for instance, allow us to retrieve documents about Tchaikovsky by entering either "Chaikovsky" or "Tchaikovsky."

Actually, most Internet agents and search engines are considerably more sophisticated than this example suggests. Internet agents and search engines routinely use morphological analysis to enhance their searching capabilities. Morphological analysis techniques automatically expand words to include all members of their inflectional and derivational sets, which substantially improves recall (Yankelovich, 1994, p. 138). In other words, if we enter the term "teacher," then Internet agents and search engines will automatically expand teacher into its many variant forms, such as "teacher, teachers, or teaching."

The use of morphological analysis techniques is simply the latest advance in the attempt to make the search engine responsible for translating the user's ideas into the querying language of the database management system. It is, thus, a recognition that it is difficult "to express ideas in a language other than one's own" (Parsaye & Chignell, 1993, p. 129). Parsaye and Chignell continue by noting that we usually know what we want to ask, but we have trouble translating our ideas into the artificial language used by traditional information retrieval systems.

As the preceding examples illustrate, today's graphical interfaces are designed for ease of use. In fact, it is only a slight exaggeration to argue that "ease of use" is the key to competitive success in the design of information retrieval systems. The short, turbulent history of the Internet illustrates just how important ease of use can be in a competitive environment. In 1992 Gopher represented a major improvement over the traditional UNIX commands, which were definitely "user-hostile." As a result, Gopher became the dominant search engine on the Internet. Two years later the undisputed king of the Internet search engines was dethroned by graphic browsers such as Netscape and Mosaic. As Nielsen (1995, p. 183) observes, "This change in market share definitely proves the importance of good user interfaces." It also proves just how rapidly change takes place in the software industry and how quickly customer expectations can change.

The Book House project offers an interesting example of how hypertext and graphic interfaces can be combined to make finding a book easier. The project was designed to help public-library customers find novels. The Book House project was conducted under the leadership of Annelise Mark Pejtersen and was field tested in Denmark (Nielsen, 1995, pp. 116–119).

Because people have many different ways of finding books, the Book House supports four different search strategies, which can be selected in the strategy selection room by clicking on one of the four areas in the room. The four search strategies are browsing, search by analogy, picture browsing, and analytic search. The simplest strategy, random browsing, takes the user directly to a random location in the books database. Selecting the picture browsing strategy takes the reader to a set of icons that represent major subjects. The exact meaning of the icons depends on whether the user has been identified by the system as a child or an adult. Each of the icons represent a set of search terms that can be selected by clicking. This approach frees the user from having to generate search terms and may also provide a tool that can help uncover vaguely perceived terms. The search terms associated with each icon were determined by empirical user testing. The search by analogy strategy prompts the user to select the book he or she has already read, and then the system will display a list of similar books, ordered by a similarity rating. The final strategy, analytic search, provides access to 12 classification dimensions: plot, physical appearance of book, genre, main characters by name, main characters by age, geographical setting, social and professional setting, readability of text, historical period, emotional experience (exciting, humorous, etc.), author, and title. Since these dimensions can be combined, users can find romance novels set in 17th-century France. The Book House also uses hypertext principles to allow users to change strategies by jumping back to the strategy selection room or by linking books "similar" to the one currently being displayed.

Field tests of the Book House have confirmed that regular library users do indeed use multiple strategies. The analytical classifications accounted for 31 percent of the searches. Picture browsing was the second most used, accounting for 27 percent. Search by analogy accounted for 23 percent of the searches, and the remaining 20 percent of the searches, used random browsing. User reactions to this system were favorable; 95 percent of the users were satisfied with the interface, and 84 percent were satisfied with the search results.

Although it is likely that the participants of the Book House study shared the tendency of participants who are involved in studies of new technology to respond favorably to novel or "high-tech" experiments, the high levels of customer satisfaction are, nevertheless, indicative that the new interface was easier to use than the conventional card catalog interface (Landauer et al., 1993, p. 87). Moreover, there is little doubt that the Book House's use of multiple search strategies clearly outperformed the conventional OPAC's subject searching capabilities by a wide margin (see Adams, 1988, p. 34; Markey, 1986, p. 60). Of course since approximately half of all subject searches on traditional OPACs "are totally unsuccessful," outperforming an OPAC is not exactly a world-class achievement.

CHANGING CUSTOMER EXPECTATIONS

> Take care of the luxuries and the necessities will take care of themselves.
> —Dorothy Parker

For today's library users, graphical interfaces have made the rapid transition from exciting innovation to expected technology. It has become the minimum level of acceptable technology. The command line interface used in OPACs, the insistence on using Boolean operators, and the need for exact matches—all these signal to the customer that the library's information retrieval system is outdated. Like it or not, the Internet is establishing standards of convenience that library customers will expect of all software—including library software.

Oddly enough, the real limitations of the Internet are almost invariably ignored by users. After all, the Internet allows home access, uses simple query languages, and has information on nearly every imaginable topic. This convenience and power has proven so seductive that few users ever question the quality, authoritativeness, or timeliness of the information found on the Net. Critics like Shapiro and Varian (1999, p. 8) are correct in pointing out that the Internet is not "all that impressive as an information resource":

> The static, publicly accessible HTML text on the Web is roughly equivalent in size to 1.5 million books. The UC Berkeley Library has 8 million volumes, and the average quality of the Berkeley library content is much, much higher! If 10 percent of the material on the Web is "useful," there are about 150,000 useful book-equivalents on it, which is about the size of a Borders superstore. But the actual figure for "useful" is probably more like 1 percent, which is 15,000 books, or half the size of an average mall bookstore.

Judging by customer acceptance, the ultimate arbiter of success, the Internet has become an enormously successful information source. Critics may rightly lament its imperfections and limitations, but they must also recognize that the public acceptance of the Internet has been overwhelming. In fact, Internet traffic continues to double every 100 days (Ohlson, 1998). If nothing else, the success of the Internet should convince library professionals that it is time to rethink our information retrieval systems.

At a minimum, library customers expect an information system to:

- Be easy to use (highly intuitive interface);
- Be interactive (immediate feedback on results);
- Use natural language queries (users should not have to translate their ideas and intentions into the database's querying language); and
- Offer powerful data analysis and manipulation tools.

Needless to say, the minimum requirements listed above are subject to change. For instance, many Internet users are already used to having intelligent software agents automatically search the Net for documents that fit their individualized interest profiles and then deliver the desired documents directly to their PC (Norman, 1998, p. 104). The obvious question for the library professional is, How long will it be before library users expect this same type of service to be available through the library?

Historically, libraries have added value for the customer by providing bibliographic citations. The actual retrieval of the documents was a separate step that was the responsibility of the customer. Once again, the Internet and online databases are changing the ground rules. An increasing number of customers now expect information retrieval systems to retrieve full-text documents and not just a list of bibliographic citations. Full-text document delivery is, of course, only today's client expectation. Voice recognition software promises to become the next revolutionary software development. In addition to very affordable prices, voice recognition software has, at last, become practical for PC users. Needless to say, once this software becomes widely distributed, library customers will expect that library information retrieval systems will also respond to voice commands.

Perhaps the greatest challenge—as well as greatest opportunity—that libraries will confront in the next decade is moving from being a passive information supplier to providing information that is organized to meet the specific needs of each customer. Once again, this major transformation is fueled by advances in information technology and software design. As a result of these advances, libraries now have, for the first time in history, the capability to meet the specific informational needs of each and every customer. In addition to retrieving the desired information, intelligent databases can also organize and structure the information to meet the unique needs of each client.

ELECTRONIC DISTRIBUTION CHANNELS AND THE
LIBRARY'S CHANGING ROLE

To maintain their readership, newspapers and magazines have had to repeatedly reinvent themselves—first to combat television's sound and light, later to do battle against sound bites, and now to meet the challenge of on-line delivery and Internet information exchange.

Blessedly, books have managed to stay above the fray. Until now. The sheer mass of information available in multiple media demands that publishers take a serious look at the needs of their readers and assess how to be of service.
—Warren Bennis, *Preface to Fabled Service*

Like books, libraries have remained largely unchanged and unchallenged—until now. The historic role of the library was to act as a distribution channel, linking the author with the reader. In a sense, all distribution channels—whatever the industry—link the producer of an item with its customer in the same way that a supermarket links the wholesaler with the retail shopper. Advances in information technology and telecommunications have revolutionized many industries by replacing the conventional distribution channels with electronic networks.

In addition to their unmatched speed, electronic distribution channels offer major cost incentives. For instance, in *Future Perfect*, Stan Davis (1987, p. 63) estimates that distribution costs constitute anywhere from 45 to 80 percent of operating costs in service businesses. By replacing the physical distribution channels—the buildings, trucks, trains, libraries, and offices—with electronic channels, companies can offer faster service at bargain prices. Because of these cost advantages, the "middleman functions between producers and consumers are being eliminated through digital networks" (Tapscott, 1996, p. 56). Agents, wholesalers, distributors, retailers, and middle managers are all at risk as disintermediation transforms entire industries (Tapscott, 1996, p. 56).

Autonetwork is an interesting example of how a network can act as a virtual warehouse. Wrecking yards and junkyards for automobiles (auto dismantlers) are in the business of selling salvageable parts. To provide a function similar to central warehousing, auto dismantlers have networked with one another since the 1950s. They began by using telephone party lines. In 1970 a small firm in California introduced electronic messaging to this industry. Two decades later this electronic network account for over $1 billion in parts sales per year (Tapscott & Caston, 1993, p. 114).

The replacement of distribution channels threatens entire industries. For example, electronic distribution channels have the ability to replace travel agents. Unless travel agents become travel consultants who can add value for their customers by delivering new and needed services, they are in danger of being replaced by electronic ticket sales. Already more than 20 percent of air travelers purchase their tickets directly from the airlines. By using networks as the distribution channel, airlines are able to move closer to the customer, thus making travel agents unnecessary. As a result, the airlines get to pocket the sales commissions that they formerly paid to travel agents.

Although the long-term prospects for travel agents appear grim, one travel agency, Summit Travel of Winston-Salem, North Carolina, has responded by developing a software package that helps travelers search the Internet for flights and then helps travelers make the transactions themselves. Since the software routes the reservation through Summit, the company has hit upon a creative method of adding value for their customers (Tapscott, 1996, p. 58).

Like the travel industry, libraries also act as intermediaries in the distribution channel. And, like all intermediaries, libraries must face the fact that in most cases, "when customers shift to electronic distribution channels, traditional channels wither" (Davis & Davidson, 1991, p. 75). While some might argue that Tapscott (1996, p. 55) is premature when he states that "the national information infrastructure has become the utility of the 21st century just as electrification and highways were the vital infrastructure of the economy in the first half of the twentieth century," only the hardiest of Luddites would disagree with his prediction in the long term.

One of the most impressive examples of how an electronic distribution channel (CD-ROMs) can replace a traditional channel (the library) is seen in the Perseus project. The Perseus project is designed to support a wide range of readers, from the freshman taking a translation course to the graduate student preparing a dissertation on Thucydides. The interface provides different views for different types of students. Perseus offers the student the original Greek passage in one window and its English translation in a second window. Clicking on a personal name takes the reader to a classical encyclopedia; clicking on geographical places calls up a map of Greece. By clicking on individual words, the student can see the term's morphological analysis. Variant readings of the text can also be retrieved with a click of the mouse.

Perseus's more advanced features clearly demonstrate the potential of hypermedia. If a student who is looking at the map of Greece wants to see more details, the zoom feature allows a subsection of the map to be seen in greater detail. Each view is also linked to one or more video images. Most video images can be displayed from multiple vantage points. For example, an archaeologist or art historian viewing the site plans of Aegina might want to zoom in to the building level and then see a written entry on the building. The user can also find other buildings of the same type or move to the Vase or Coin Index to see what vases or coins come from Aegina.

When completed, the Perseus project will contain the most important texts that survive from Homer to Plato. It will also provide atlases and maps for all of the major classical sites. The Perseus project will also take advantage of the multimedia capability of digital databases by providing digital images of art objects, such as statues and vases that not only illustrate the major currents of artistic creation but cover iconography as well. By collecting tragedies, maps, lyric poems, vases, histories, statues, coins, and other materials in a single medium, students and researchers will be able to move from one type of information to another with the click of a mouse button.

The student or researcher can easily widen or narrow the scope of material retrieved so that rather than focusing only on the relevant material that happens to appear in the manuscripts of Greek comedies the study can also incorporate architectural plans. The Perseus project's ability to seamlessly incorporate many kinds of materials will, in turn, allow researchers to take advantage of as many kinds of evidence as possible. Yankelovitch (1994, p. 215) notes that certain types of materials can best be captured in digital formats:

We cannot simply replicate the forms of printed reference works—nor should we want to. An art book can contain at most several hundred black and white images and several dozen good color prints, but a CD-ROM can store thousands of color images.

Although the Perseus project employs CD-ROM technology rather than the Internet to disseminate information, it clearly illustrates how information technology can dramatically alter the ways in which scholars and students access materials. In the case of the Perseus project, information technology, hypertext, and CD-ROM storage have been combined to provide a hint of some of the ways that an intelligent knowledge base could provide access and levels of service that simply are impossible using print-based media. It is one more indicator of the correctness of Michael Porter and Victor Millar's (1985, p. 160) prediction that:

The importance of the information revolution is not in dispute. The question is not whether information technology will have a significant impact on a company's competitive position; rather the question is when and how this impact will strike. Companies that anticipate the power of information technology will be in control of events. Companies that do not respond will be forced to accept changes that other initiate and will find themselves at a competitive disadvantage.

So far, the experience of commercial firms with electronic channels has made it quite clear that "when existing industry participants neglect the information dimensions of their business, for whatever reasons, independent third parties emerge to fill this role" (Davis & Davidson, 1991, p. 96). The evidence also indicates that not all companies will make the transition; in fact, many will not survive because they will fail to reconfigure their businesses around the new technologies (Davis & Davidson, 1991, p. 63). In other words, if libraries do not adapt themselves so as to take full advantage of information technology and electronic distribution channels, "the big research libraries and their great buildings will go," in the words of Robert Zich, "the way of the railroad stations and the movie palaces of an earlier era" (quoted in Weeks, 1991, p. 30).

Because wealth is increasingly "based on knowledge and on the ability to use that knowledge," libraries can expect increasing competition from the public sector (Handy, 1989, p. 141). The Internet is already teeming with fledgling enterprises that offer rapid access to specialized information. For example, ESPN Sports offers in-depth statistical analyses for every major team in the United States. For a modest fee, the sports fan can obtain the kind of detailed information that was previously limited to scouting combines. Amazon.com furnishes book reviews from more than 50 sources, including the *NY Times Book Review*, *Wired*, *Atlantic*, *The New Yorker*, the *Wall Street Journal*, and National Public Radio.

For the serious investor, there is a bewildering array of Web sites clamoring for the privilege of providing up-to-date financial information that covers the Dow Jones, the European markets, the bond markets, and high-tech stocks. Again, in this arena the Internet offers access to financial information that no library system could ever match. These examples could, of course, be duplicated in literally hundreds of other fields in which for-profit organizations provide the kind of specialized information that is simply beyond the scope and ken of libraries. Because information has truly become "the key resource of the twenty-first century" (Parsaye & Chignell, 1993, p. 512), it was inevitable that new information intensive organizations would increasingly dominate the economy and would increasingly replace many of the libraries as a source of high-quality information with commercial value.

Although it would be easy to conjure up doomsday scenarios in which libraries would be replaced by digital networks, this prediction ignores one simple fact: Libraries will continue to be needed, if only to archive materials that are out of print and not considered important enough to be converted into a digital format (De Gennaro, 1987, p. 55; Landauer, 1993 et al., p. 11). The role of library in society would, however, be so marginalized that the library would be reduced to serving as the final resting place for all of the books and journals that possess no economic value. In effect, the library would become the dumping ground for materials so marginal that no other organization considers them worthwhile to preserve.

THE CHALLENGE AND THE OPPORTUNITY

The future of the library becomes even more problematic when we realize that libraries must now compete with other social agencies for increasingly scarce funding. As the competition for public revenue sources increases, libraries of all types face increasing pressures to become more accountable and more customer-oriented. In today's competitive environment, it has become painfully obvious that "nothing is more dangerous to the long-term health of an organization than 'business as usual'" (Band, 1991, p. 180). Like so many organizations, libraries find it difficult "to face the truth about themselves" (Ackoff, 1981, p. 85). It becomes even more difficult when an organization that has been successful for many years is asked to change the very factors that made it successful in the first place. For an institution steeped in traditional values, such as the library, the urge to cling to the old formulas that brought success in the past is well nigh irresistible.

As we see in the next chapter, intelligent databases and their close relative, hypermedia knowledge-bases, offer the library profession powerful tools that can be used to provide individualized customer services that will go far toward making the library a viable institution in the next century.

8

The New Alexandrian Library: Libraries and Information Management

There is a tide in the affairs of men, Which, taken at the flood, leads on to fortune,
On such a full sea we are now afloat, And we must take the current when it serves,
Or lose our ventures.
—William Shakespeare, *Julius Caesar*

It is safe to say that the World Wide Web is simultaneously
overhyped and undervalued.
—Jeff Papows

THE DIGITAL LIBRARY: OPPORTUNITY AND THREAT

The great conundrum facing librarians is what to do with the power of the networked computer. The Internet clearly opens up enormous possibilities for nearly every organization, especially information-centered organizations such as libraries. How to transform this power to meet customer needs and expectations is the pressing problem of recent years for the library professional.

The role of the Internet in business is equally fuzzy. About the only certainty is that "a corporate presence on the Internet is now a necessity" (Sterne, 1999, p. xxi). For starters, the Internet "has even been credited with being a major cause of the United States' economic strength of the late 1990s," and "even the Asian economic crisis couldn't put a damper on the continued growth of the U.S. economy, spawned by a new marketplace called the Web" (p. xxi).

For the jaded observer of the computer industry, such claims can be dismissed as yet another extravagant and unsubstantiated claim. When it is realized that no less an authority than Alan Greenspan has attributed the United States' extraordinary economic success to the $2 trillion investment in information technology by U.S. firms, it strongly suggests that the often predicted digital economic revolution has finally become a fact instead of a forecast (Papows, 1998, p. 1). The magnitude of the impending change can be seen by examining some basic figures about the U.S. economy: First, an estimated 42 percent of the investment capital in the U.S. now goes into information technology; second, more than 35 percent of the growth in the U.S. GDP during the last six years has been associated with growth in information technology (p. 3).

Even the often ballyhooed electronic commerce showed definite signs of becoming an economic reality. Margaret Kane (1998) reported that "1998 will be remembered as the year that Internet commerce began to deliver upon some of its lofty promises with holiday sales over the Internet reaching approximately $2.3 billion"— a figure which made the U.S. Commerce Department's April 1998 prediction that electronic commerce would grow to a $300 billion a year industry by 2002 far more believable (Sterne, 1999, p. 23). For one CNN business analyst, 1998 was the year that "e-commerce, e-business, I-commerce, Netbiz—whatever it has been called over the years" finally "changed the world" (Tweney, 1999).

The simple truth is that as more people come online—an estimated 150 million users by the end of 1999—the Internet is too big and too powerful for companies to ignore. As the commercial Web enters its fifth year, even previously skeptical firms such as Coca-Cola, Xerox, Johnson & Johnson, Unilever, and DaimlerChrysler have decided that they can no longer afford to neglect the commercial possibilities of the Internet (Weaver, 1998).

At the heart of the digital revolution lies one powerful idea, which Jeff Papows (1998, p. 5) summarizes as follows: "The time will come—sooner rather than later—when an enterprise's primary connection to the outside world will be its World Wide Web site and its collaborative and messaging-reliant extensions." Papows (1998, p. xi) continues:

> It is my conviction that we are in the early years of a fundamental change in the way that our civilization works. Seemingly basic conventions and terminology such as customers, communities, culture, and even competitors will take on new meaning as we begin to come to grips with the truly borderless, twenty-four-hour world enabled by today's technology.

CHALLENGE OF THE DIGITAL LIBRARY

> Companies must be ever watchful, to the point of paranoia, for sudden,
> technology-driven, categorical transformations that threaten not only their products
> but the very way they do business.
> —Andrew Grove

The early warning signs that libraries have lost their 2,000-year-old monopoly on information storage and retrieval are not difficult to find. Stephen L. Talbott (1995, p. 11) cites one popular view about the advantages of electronic media:

> Print journals are now valid as historical records rather than as the primary source of new information. If a particular field does not have ejournals [electronic journals], I believe that the researchers in that field are falling behind. The immediacy of the research in these fields could be questioned. Many fields are moving so quickly, that anyone not involved in electronic exchanges on their research would be out of it.

Although Talbott (1995, p. 11) dismisses this view as "arrogant nonsense, however often repeated," it is a clear warning that the World Wide Web has changed the way many individuals go about looking for information. Jim Sterne (1999, p. 33), in his book *World Wide Web Marketing*, sketched out the following scenarios, which attempt to capture how the Internet has changed the rules for finding information.

Prior to the Web, our mythical customer, Fred, walks into the library and stops at the reference desk to look for statistics on commerce in Oregon. As expected, Fred finds a multitude of books that appear to contain some of the information that he wants. During the next two weeks, Fred eventually finds the key publications that contain the most complete and current references on Oregon business.

After the Web, Fred logs into the Internet and goes straight to Yahoo!. Yahoo! quickly locates a multitude of sites that are relevant to his search. Many of the Web sites contain some of the information he is searching for. They also contain numerous links to other sites that might be helpful. In the next few days, Fred surfs the Web sites and prints out those sites that are especially useful. In addition to the usual text-based documents, Fred also finds an audio recording from the governor outlining the state's industrial policy. He locates a satellite photo highlighting Oregon's waterways, plus photos of individual towns. He also downloads charts depicting the population density of specific regions in the state as well as a clip of a helicopter flight along the coastline.

While this example of searching on the Web is obviously biased—at least in the eyes of many library professionals—it is important to note that most Web users are not cognizant that the Web is not necessarily the best possible information source. For a start, most users overlook that the quality of information on the Web varies enormously. As McKinley (1997, p. 62) notes, "On the Web, geniuses and charlatans have equal access." Usability studies have repeatedly found; "If you give people a specific problem to solve on the Web, they will only rarely succeed in arriving at the correct solution" (Rosenfeld & Morville, 1998, p. xi).

However, despite its real limitations as an information source, the Web remains a convenient and deceptively easy means of locating information. In fact, the Web is so easy and so convenient that it has become the fastest-growing information source in the world. Douglas E. Comer (1997, p. 277), one of the architects of the Internet, is absolutely correct when he writes: "The Internet is a wildly successful, rapidly-growing, global digital library built on a remarkably flexible communications technology."

To dismiss the Internet as a limited source of information may be accurate in some respects, but it is also very dangerous. We must remember that traffic on the Internet doubled every year from 1989 to 1995. And after 1995 the rate of growth became even more rapid (Shapiro & Varian, 1999, p. 13). For better or worse, the Internet is perceived as being easy, perhaps even, fun to use. The image of the library, on the other hand, is often closer to Landauer's (1995, p. 363) disturbing, albeit insightful, description:

> How many times did teachers tell you that all you need to know is how to use the library? Did you believe them? Did you stop studying textbooks and just rely on visiting the library? No. Using the library is too hard, slow, and unreliable.

In many respects our professional critique of the Internet has disturbing echoes of the same blend of snobbery and condescension that was, in part, responsible for the rapid decline of the finest encyclopedia in the world. To the amazement of many, "the encyclopedia Britannica as we knew it is no more" (Rosenberg, 1997, p. 1F). "Instead the 32-volume citadel of Western knowledge, launched by a pair of Scots in 1768, is quietly fading before the onslaught of computer technology" (p. 1F). Britannica's chief operating officer, James E. Goulka, "freely admits that Britannica was slow to adapt to the new age." As a result, Britannica watched its revenues slip by more than one third—from $658 million in 1991 to $423 million in 1995 (p. 3F). Goulka states that Britannica was "asleep at the switch when computers entered the market beginning in the 1990s" (p. 3F).

Despite its unquestioned excellence, consumers overwhelmingly selected Microsoft's inexpensive and very convenient CD-ROM-based encyclopedia, Encarta. Although the quality and depth of Britannica's essays remain unmatched by any of its competitors, the digital upstarts such as Encarta are the clear winners in the encyclopedia sweepstakes. Today there is no longer a paper-based version of the Britannica; it exists only on CDs and the Internet. While there were many reasons for Britannica's dramatic eclipse, at least part of the reason was given by Jim Neeley, a librarian at the University of Kansas, who observes: "There is no question that students much prefer electronic resources to print resources" (Rosenberg, 1997, p. 3F).

INCREASING COMPETITION FOR LIBRARIES

> Many things indicate that we are going through a transitional period when it seems
> that something is on the way out and something else is painfully being born.
> —Václav Havel

> In a few years, libraries as we know them will start to disappear, and information
> will be found on "the Net."
> —Douglas E. Comer (1995)

Rather than focus on the Web's limitations as an information retrieval system, it seems far more prudent to examine the reasons why the Web has become such a success story. According to McKinley (1997, p. 247), "most users come to the Web hoping to find an easier way of accessing information." In a very revealing passage, McKinley (p. 234) notes that because of their experience with the Internet, user expectations have already changed significantly:

> The user thinks: "If I am going to a digital library, I expect to be able to search every single word in every book in the whole library. Otherwise I could just go to the old library with the paper card catalog."

Perhaps the best summary of the public's changing perception of the library can be found in Danny Goodman's (1994, p. 146) nostalgic look back at libraries:

> Those of us who grew up with respect and admiration for the public library's rows and rows of books, volumes of periodicals, and quiet refuge from the outside world may feel it a shame that the institutions as we knew them may disappear over time. In their place will be electronic access to the same—if not better—information. To be utilitarian about it, a library is a warehouse of information. If we can retrieve that same information, not just plain text but complete pages, on high-resolution video screens, at any time of the day or night from our homes or offices, the edifice of the library building becomes irrelevant.

Goodman (1994, p. 146) clearly views libraries with genuine affection; however, even this friend of libraries believes that when materials from many libraries are stored on one virtual computer "that lets us search for information across many disciplines and lines of thought, then the library we remember will seem like a horse carriage in a world of supersonic aircraft."

Before we succumb to nostalgia, it is important to note that with the exception of heavily subsidized college and research libraries, most libraries have already conceded their role as society's information manager, seeking to maintain their existence by becoming a marginalized provider of popular entertainment. Paul Gilster's (1997, p. 155) comments about his local public library are representative of how a majority of public libraries have tried to become consumer-oriented:

Raleigh has largely given up on the public library. Living here, I've learned that circulation numbers, not quality, are used to determine which books to put on the library shelf. Older volumes are sold off in a merciless triage operation every year, to finance the purchase of multiple copies of the latest best-sellers for each of the Wake County branch libraries. Needless to say, reference services dwindle while romance novels and celebrity biographies proliferate.

In a real sense, the Raleigh Public Library has chosen to add value for the customer by providing "free" books, records, and audiotapes. After all, that is what the customer wants, and without customers, libraries would have no reason to exist. Admittedly, the decision to become the low-cost provider of best sellers makes good political sense—in the short run. Of course, in this era of deregulation, public librarians can only hope that no one asks if the costs of providing the same materials would be cheaper if the local community subsidized the local bookstore or amazon.com instead of the public library.

But the real point is that libraries have already begun to lose their position as the public information provider. Rather than go into the entertainment or retail business, it makes far more sense for librarians to seek to add value for their clients by reassuming their traditional role of adding value for their community and society by serving as the information provider and manager of information. This option is feasible because digital technological advances now make it possible for the library to become society's knowledge manager. Needless to say, this transformation will be neither easy nor painless.

MASTER RULE: ADD VALUE FOR THE CUSTOMER

> In a knowledge business, knowledge and information are the raw materials,
> and the assets are loyal customers and employees.
> —Fred Reichhold, Service manager of Bain & Company

If the old rules and practices are increasingly less reliable and less relevant, the library profession needs a new way to think about how we can transform the library into an effective institution that will continue to play an important role in society. There is a growing agreement in management literature that the key to long-term success (or even survival) can be summarized in one short phrase: Win and keep "the customer's business by doing the right things outstandingly well" (Albrecht, 1992, p. ix). In other words, the master rule for survival in a world beset by relentless change is to add value for the customer. Of course, this axiom is deceptively simple. In practice, it has proven to be a most difficult and demanding task. For instance, if we assume that adding value for the customer should be the guiding principle that underlies our long-term strategy, we must then begin to learn how to identify what the customer perceives as "value." Next, we must attempt to devise new systems that will deliver added value that the customer will appreciate. For librarians this means that we can no longer equate the quality of a library with the size of the library's collection. Instead, we must adopt C. West Churchman's (1979, p. 112) viewpoint that "the true benefit of an information system must be measured in terms of the meaning of information for the user." At a minimum, a library organized around the principle of adding value for the customer would:

- Deal with information overload and complexity;
- Minimize time and effort required to the library.
- Deal with each customer on a one-to-one basis;
- Retrieve ideas, not citations;
- Aid customers in understanding the key interrelationships in complex disciplines;
- Encourage critical thinking;
- Act as the client's personal assistant;
- Focus on knowledge, not data;
- Be easy and pleasant to use;
- Be committed to understanding current needs and anticipating future customer needs;
- Provide tools that support critical thinking; and
- Retrieve information anywhere, anytime, and in any format.

Three of the profession's most respected voices (Stoffle, Renaud, & Veldof, 1996, p. 220) warn that for libraries to become customer-focused would require major changes in library operations:

> Libraries must move from defining quality by the size of the inputs—and especially from valuing staff and collection size as "goods" in and of themselves. They must get away from an internal professional evaluation of quality rooted in the context of what librarians agree that libraries do. All services and activities must be viewed through the eyes of the customers, letting customers determine quality by whether their needs have been satisfied.

The authors continue by noting that librarians must be prepared to abandon many cherished activities and "institute new services and programs in very short time cycles" (Stoffle et al., 1996, p. 220). Unfortunately, libraries have been slow to recognize the opportunities presented by the Internet for a variety of reasons. Rosenfeld and Morville (1998, p. xiv) believe that "many librarians have responded slowly to new information technologies like the Web because many librarians understandably fear that their clients will bypass the library and go directly to the source via the Internet." While such a fear is understandable, the truth is "that skills in information organization and access are more and more necessary in this era of information explosion" (Rosenfeld & Morville, 1998, p. xiv).

To further complicate matters, librarians must not merely focus on the current needs of their customers; they must also focus on the customer's future needs because "those future needs are not going to be the same as current or past needs, thanks to technological changes" (Burrus & Gittines, 1993, p. 29). Because customer needs are so dynamic, the library must conduct an ongoing dialogue with each of its customers in order to understand and anticipate patron needs (Peppers & Rogers, 1993, p. 77).

USER NEEDS: INFORMATION OVERLOAD

> The only thing worse than having too little information is having too much information.
> —Larry Kahaner, *Competitive Intelligence*

> Information has now become a form of garbage. We don't know what to do with it, have no control over it, don't know how to get rid of it.
> —Neil Postman

Historically, an increase in available information has been a powerful means of sustaining and developing culture. More information and better communications "have made us steadily healthier, wealthier, more tolerant" (Schenk, 1997, p. 27). But around 1945 "we crossed an important rubicon: We began to produce information much faster than we could process it" (pp. 27–28).

In fact, the amount of information available is now so large that increases in the total store of information are unimportant because civilization can generate information at a rate that transcends anyone's ability to comprehend it all (for example, in about five minutes, modern accelerator experiments generate data equivalent to the contents of the original Alexandrian library) (Robertson, 1998, pp. 22–23).

Although our ability to generate and recall data and information has been greatly enhanced by information technology, our ability to understand and process information remains no better than it was a century ago. Our plight is elegantly summarized by Mitroff and Linstone (1993, p. 20):

> Almost without exception, all who write about the new, global information age acknowledge that we are literally drowning in an overload and overabundance of information. Never before has humankind had access to so much, so quickly, and from every part of the globe. We have more data and information on every conceivable subject, yet less understanding at the same time. Data and information do not automatically lead to greater insight; they may now travel at the speed of light, but understanding and wisdom do not.

The fundamental problem, note Spitzer and Evans (1997, p. 104) is that our ability to generate vast amounts of data has far outstripped our ability to convert it into information. The gap between the speed of data collection and the speed of conversion to information is another example—maybe the prime example—of a technological capability exceeding the human capability to use the technology effectively.

COSTS OF INFORMATION OVERLOAD

> Insanity is often the logic of an accurate mind overtaxed.
> —Oliver Wendell Holmes, Jr.

> Information networks straddle the world. Nothing remains concealed. But the sheer volume of information dissolves the information. We are unable to take it all in.
> —Günter Grass

The problem of information overload promises to become even worse because within a short time "virtually all of the information produced by our civilization will be available . . .. Every individual will have instant access to a supply of information that will dwarf even the Library of Congress" (Robertson, 1998, p. 24). Although we may have access to vast amounts of information, there is no guarantee that having access to ever increasing amounts of information will prove valuable. In fact, there is an impressive body of evidence that "too much information can actually hurt" the quality of decision making (Russo & Schoemaker, 1989, p. 113). Although the reason why experienced decisionmakers often perform worse when given additional information remains poorly understood, numerous research studies have found that providing additional information can lower the performance of the decisionmaker (see Mayer, 1992, and Simon, 1997, for details).

The critical need in the coming decade and the library's great mission is to develop the software and hardware needed to make effective use of such a wealth of information. Dealing with information overload remains central to the library's regaining its historic mission of serving as society's information manager. Although we are far from completely solving the "infoglut" problem, powerful tools are already in existence that promise to bring about dramatic improvements in the ways that we store and access information. Fortunately, software advances now give us a greatly improved "ability to manipulate information." Indeed, Shapiro and Varian (1999, p. 9) note that "in every industry we see dramatic changes in technology that allow people to do more with the same information." The task of the library professional is to translate this new power into improved, customer-oriented retrieval systems.

LIBRARY AS INFORMATION MANAGER

> The real issue for future technology does not appear to be production of
> information, and certainly not transmission. Almost anybody can add information.
> The difficult question is how to reduce it.
> —Eli Noam

In essence the information overload problem really consists of two distinct problems. The first, and most obvious, is the problem of locating a desired item from millions of similar documents. It was this problem that libraries solved by organizing materials according to subject, title, or author. Unfortunately, the sheer volume of documents has strained the traditional bibliographic tools to the breaking point. In *How the Mind Works*, Steven Pinker (1997, p. 142) vividly captures the limitations of the traditional library systems:

> In an optimally designed information-retrieval system, an item should be recovered
> only when the relevance of the item outweighs the cost of retrieving it. Anyone who
> has used a computerized library retrieval system quickly comes to rue the avalanche
> of titles spilling across the screen. A human expert, despite our allegedly feeble powers
> of retrieval, vastly outperforms any computer in locating a piece of information from
> its content. When I need to find articles on a topic in an unfamiliar field, I don't use
> the library, I send email to a pal in the field.

It is no longer enough for our information retrieval systems to locate the information that matches our search terms. We now must ask our retrieval systems to "provide only the information most likely to be useful at the time of the request" (Pinker, 1997, p. 143). Pinker suggests that we could improve our retrieval systems if they incorporated some of the rules that human memory uses to retrieve facts. As we will see in a later section, recent advances in neural networks offer us powerful new tools to add these as well as other advanced techniques to our retrieval systems.

The second, and in many respects even more serious, problem stemming from information overload is our inability to understand or comprehend the torrents of information that we try to wade through in our daily life. To deal with this problem will require us to design our libraries so that they enhance our ability to learn in the same way that language, writing, and numbering systems allow us to perform mental feats that would be impossible for us to perform without the aid of artificial thinking tools—what Norman refers to as "cognitive artifacts" (1993, p. 123). In other words, we need to transform our libraries into personal assistants that, like Bush's Memex, will provide immediate access to desired information and act as a tool that helps us think and learn. Such libraries would, in fact, be intelligent knowledge-bases.

SOFTWARE AGENTS: THE DIGITAL ASSISTANT

> There is no desire more natural than the desire for knowledge.
> We try all the ways that can lead us to it.
> —Michel de Montaigne

> Information may be accumulated in files,
> but it must be retrieved to be of use in decision making.
> —Kenneth J. Arrow, *The Limits of Organization*

As we have seen, traditional retrieval systems suffer from serious and fundamental problems that severely limit their ability to identify and retrieve needed information. Because of the inherent limitations of traditional indexing methods, it is extremely difficult to find what we need when we try to search large distributed systems. In addition, the systems are rigid and inflexible; they handle simple tasks well, but they are poorly designed to cope with complex tasks (Bradshaw, 1997, p. 15). Even more fundamental, traditional retrieval systems are unable to "notice" or "learn" about a customer's needs and tastes. Consequently, we suffer from the paradoxical condition cleverly captured by John Gall in the following passage (1988, p. 107): "The information you have is not the information you want. The information you want is not the information you need. The information you need is not the information you can obtain."

What is clearly needed is a new type of interface that could learn about each customer's specific needs and then meet those needs. Intelligent software agents have the potential to overcome the rigidity and inflexibility of traditional computer interfaces.

"Software agent" is really an umbrella term that covers a wide range of software. Nwana (1996, pp. 205–207), for instance, has categorized software agents into seven groups: collaborative agents, interface agents, mobile agents, information/Internet agents, reactive agents, hybrid agents, and smart agents. Whatever name we use for them, intelligent software agents are computer programs that have the ability to "simulate a human relationship by doing something that another person could otherwise do for you" (Cheong, 1996, p. 5). Granted, their ability "to simulate a human relationship" is quite limited. However, software agents already have the capability to run background searches at specific times or even respond automatically to system events (such as date or time). Like Negroponte's digital butler (Negroponte, 1995), they can filter, extract, and present "the relevant information from bodies of information larger than we could ordinarily digest" on our own (Bradshaw, 1997, p. 20). And since software agents can be designed to share our goals rather than simply process our commands, they "can find ways to 'work around' unforeseen problems and exploit new opportunities as they help solve problems" (Bradshaw, 1997, p. 17).

There are already many examples of how software agents can improve information access. Yankelovich (1994, p. 137), for instance, discusses one type of agent that is already popularized by Amazon.com. This agent routinely searches new documents to see if they match the client's interest profile. When new items are found that match the customer's interests, the agent automatically sends an e-mail message to the customer that lists all of the documents deemed relevant by the agent. Amazon.com's agents not only send the e-mail message, but the e-mail message contains hypertext links to the original document so that the customer only has to click on the link to call up the relevant documents. Of course, this use of agents is really just an updating of traditional SDI services.

A much more interesting capability of software agents, however, is their ability to learn about our needs. By using learning algorithms, software agents can, over time, improve their performance by gradually building up an understanding of the needs of the user. The feedback can be collected directly from the user or simply by seeing when the user ignores the agent's suggested action (Cheong, 1996, p. 24). By noticing recurrent patterns and actions, the software can eventually improve its competence so that "over time, the agents become more helpful as they accumulate knowledge about how the user handles certain situations" (p. 7).

Interestingly enough, the new generation of software agents will not be designed to solve complex problems by themselves Instead, the agents will be designed so that the boundary between what the agents do and what the humans do remains flexible (Bradshaw, 1997, p. 23). Although the search engines are still relatively primitive, they still represent a major improvement over traditional search interfaces, and the next generation will be so much better that Fah-Chun Cheong predicts that the new breed of agents will radically transform human–computer interfaces (1996, p. 78).

THE ONE-TO-ONE CUSTOMER RELATIONSHIP

Global competition will segment markets into finer slices.
—Chuck Martin (1999)

If marketing is seminally about anything, it is about achieving customer-getting distinction by differentiating what you do and how you operate. To differentiate an offering effectively requires knowing what drives and attracts customers. It requires knowing how customers differ from one another and how those differences can be clustered into commercially meaningful segments. If you're not thinking segments, you're not thinking.
—Theodore Levitt (1986)

We now have the technology to customize products and services to the individual. One person—one market. So the trick for the marketing executive of the future is to know how to build products and services which can be tweaked to the exact

needs and desires of the individual.
—Annie Brooking, *Corporate Memory*

Since software agents can modify their actions to meet the customer's needs, they are a prime example of how the digital revolution gives us the power to customize service. One of the hallmarks of the intelligent knowledge-base will be its ability to address individual needs. From the client's perspective, the system will actually be configured for his or her individual preferences. By offering individualized service, the library will be able to adapt its services to the customer instead of attempting to make the client adapt to the library's services.

The ability to offer customized service is seen by most marketing mavens as an essential competitive tool (see Allen, Kania, & Yaeckel, 1998; Bayne, 1997; Judson, 1996; Martin, 1999; Mougayar, 1997; Peppers & Rodgers, 1997; and Sterne, 1999). As Davis recognized a decade ago, the importance of individualized service can be captured by the following question: "If given the choice between a standardized and a customized product at the same price, which would you choose?" (1987, p. 166). Obviously, the ability to deliver individualized service is an enormous competitive advantage. Once again, Amazon.com's notification system allows each customer to ask the system to send an e-mail message when a book is published on a particular subject or by a particular author. Such a system is, of course, fairly primitive when compared to the next generation of customized service, which will employ software agents to provide truly individualized service.

THE CRITICAL RESOURCE

Professionals have found themselves on "information overload" and starved for knowledge—the downside of a technologically sophisticated society. The challenge then is to develop mechanisms to ensure that time—the most precious commodity of all—is spent on genuine value-added activities.
—Debra Amidon

Not only will intelligent software agents provide customized service, but they also will save the most valuable and critical resource of the information age: time. In the following passage, Crawford (1991, p. 83) summarizes the reasons for this development:

Similarly, in an industrial society the accumulation of personal wealth is the principal means for social advancement, whereas, in the knowledge society social status is derived increasingly from knowledge and personal achievement rather than personal wealth, a change that reflects the principal scarcity in a knowledge society—time, not goods.

One of the axioms of the information age is that time has such a great intrinsic value that any feature that will save time for the client will be prized. Time is the currency of the information age. In the words of Esther Dyson (1998):

> We're moving toward a culture where everything moves faster, where no one has any time, where we measure out our days not in coffee spoons but in emails, beeper buzzes, timed phone calls, children's scheduled play dates, and vacations with cell phone and laptop at hand.

NEURAL NETWORKS

Another new technology that offers dramatic possibilities for improving retrieval is neural networking. After discounting the inevitable hyperbole, there is no doubt that neural networks can dramatically improve our ability to recall and analyze certain types of data. At present the technology has considerable promise for recognizing patterns and discovering previously unknown relationships in large collections of data (Bigus, 1996, p. xiv). Neural networks are already being used by businesses as a tool for data mining.

Neural networks and data mining techniques are often effective in cases where "traditional programmed applications cannot be developed, since no one in the business understands how the data relates well enough to design or write an algorithm to capture these relationships" (Bigus, 1996, p. 16). Other areas in which neural networks have been successfully used are in solving constraint and optimization problems by using weighted connections (fuzzy logic instead of Boolean logic); problems that have multiple or conflicting goals; and clustering and classification problems (p. 40). Exactly how important the role of neural networks will be remains open to debate. Nevertheless, there is no doubt that they have already established themselves as a useful and powerful data analysis tool. If nothing else, neural networks demonstrate how the formerly staid world of information retrieval is now undergoing rapid changes and how advances in software design are opening up new possibilities.

Although neural networks have been limited to business applications, they would obviously be useful to library clients in many situations. Clients who face an optimization problem such as wanting to get the most value for their money when they buy a car or a home often find the process so complicated that they cannot rationally compare the tradeoffs. Because neural networks are designed to mine large amounts of data and then make tradeoffs based on clients' criteria, they would be an ideal tool for helping clients with such complex decisions.

THE LIBRARY AS A TOOL FOR LEARNING

If little else, the brain is an educational toy.
—Tom Robbins

The most effective way to cope with the enormous amount of information is to ignore most of it. Rather than hurrying from one idea to the next, we should begin asking more fundamental questions.
—Bo Dahlbom and Lars Mathiassen, *Computers in Context*

Nearly 20 years ago, Russell Ackoff pointed out that one of the serious side effects of information overload is that it can interfere with learning. In fact, Ackoff (1981, p. 140) notes:

Most of us who have suffered from an information overload are aware of the fact that when the amount of information exceeds a certain amount, a supersaturation point, both the amount and percentage of it that we try to absorb decreases. We give up hope of being able to keep up and abandon our efforts to do so. The more we get beyond this point the less we use.

Jakob Nielsen (1995, p. 219) has even suggested that in a world with too much information, "one also needs to consider the negative value of information in terms of the resources spent reading or pondering it." All too often our information retrieval systems interfere with the learning process by inundating us with unstructured information. The key term here is "unstructured." When dealing with random numbers, for instance, George A. Miller (1956, pp. 93–96) found that the short-term memory is limited to five to nine bits of information at a time.

Building on Miller's work, Newell and Simon (1972) argue that thinking, problem solving, and decision making are largely dependent on the contents of primary (short-term) memory. Their claim implies that our thinking and decisions can be affected by only a few factors at a time "unless we find some conscious way to summarize the impact of some of the factors that we cannot hold in memory at one time (Baron, 1994, p. 76). "The limitations on primary memory," Baron writes, "seem to place an important constraint on thinking, especially in novel situations where we have not developed extensive methods for 'chunking' information."

At first glance, our short-term memory performance seems to represent a major limitation on our mental prowess. Donald A. Norman (1993, p. 43) argues that, in general:

The power of the unaided mind is highly overrated, without external aids, memory, thought, and reasoning are all constrained but human intelligence is highly flexible and adaptive, superb at inventing procedures and objects that overcome its own limits. The real powers come from devising external aids that enhance cognitive abilities.

> How have we increased memory, thought, and reasoning? By the invention of external
> aids: It is things that make us smart.

Historically, the most important of our external aids have been paper and pencil allied to the corresponding skills of reading and writing (Norman, 1993, p. 44). Of course, the human mind is capable of storing far more information if the information makes sense and has a pattern. Larkin et al. (1980, p. 1342) found that the differences between experts and novices in solving physics problems revolves around patterns. The expert is mentally guided by a large number of patterns serving as an index to relevant parts of a knowledge store. Larkin et al. speculate that this capacity to use patterns is probably a large part of what is called physical intuition.

The ability of a chess master is perhaps the most impressive example of how greatly the structure of information can affect our ability to remember. For instance, "chess masters are able to reconstruct a board position of more than 20 pieces after only five seconds study, but only if the position is legal; for randomly positioned pieces the chess masters perform no better than novices" (Hammond, 1993, pp. 57–58).

Since chess masters reputedly have superb visual memories, their surprising inability to outperform chess novices when the pieces were arranged randomly dramatically underscores (Parsaye & Chignell, 1993, p. 71) that:

> One of the weaknesses of the human mind is in handling lots of details. One of its
> strengths is detecting patterns and seeing correspondences and links between things
> that are objectively very different. Tools that allow people to combine and interrelate
> information are very important.

Since the mind is particularly adept at detecting patterns, it comes as no surprise that current theory postulates that people organize the knowledge they have about the world into schemas (Campbell, 1989, p. 90). Campbell defines a "schema" as a generalized "structure of existing knowledge that is used to process and interpret new information." In fact, schemas play a fundamental role in human learning. Schank and Cleary (1995, p. 49) state that, "When people learn, when they build knowledge, they are either creating new schemas, or linking together preexisting schemas in new ways." Schemas also explain why we have so much trouble learning random facts or making sense out of unstructured information.

It turns out that facts are only half of what we require when we try to learn something. The other half of learning involves creating links to schemas that translate the new facts into knowledge. "Before we can absorb new background knowledge we must understand to what that knowledge relates" (Schank & Cleary, 1995, p. 62). "What individuals see in the outside world," writes van der Heijden (1996, p. 116), "is determined by the schemas and concepts they use."

Our heavy reliance on schemas to comprehend and understand the world around us explains why we are so ill equipped to deal with large amounts of unorganized and unstructured data. In fact, the mind, according to Crowell, Caine, and Caine (1998, p. 8), "resists having meaninglessness imposed on it." They define "meaningless" as "isolated pieces of information." Unfortunately, their definition could also apply to the results of most online searches. Clearly, one way to improve our ability to deal with large amounts of information is to provide some form of pattern or context that allows our minds to translate large amounts of information into a meaningful pattern. There is a great deal of evidence that indicates that "the difficult part of learning is forming the right conceptual structure" (Norman, 1993, p. 28). According to David Jonassen (1993, p. 164), "What matters most in learning is the construction of personally relevant knowledge structures."

What is needed is to design our information retrieval systems so that they not only locate desired items, but they will display the information to the client in ways that help clients fold the new information into their personal schemas. Although no single organizational pattern will work, we will discuss one possible method of supplying context and meaning to an information retrieval system. By showing the patterns in the information, we will make the retrieved information more meaningful, which will help speed up the process of acquiring and understanding information. Of course, speeding up the learning process will add enormous value for our customers because "the ultimate 'limits to growth' of knowledge and wisdom" is time (Cleveland, 1991, p. 30). As we mentioned earlier, time has become the critical resource in the information age, which is why "almost all technology today is focused on compressing to zero the amount of time it takes to acquire and use information, to learn, to make decisions, to initiate action, to deploy resources, to innovate" (McKenna, 1997, p. 4).

SCHEMA FRIENDLY RETRIEVAL

Society must learn to learn faster.
—Eric K. Drexler

People who do not educate themselves, and keep reeducating themselves, to participate in the new knowledge environment will be the peasants of the information society. And societies that do not give all their people a chance at a relevant education, and also periodic opportunities to tune up their knowledge and their insights, will be left in the jetstream of history by those that do.
—Harlan Cleveland

While there are many possible ways in which we could attempt to add context and meaning to our retrieval systems, the method chosen is relatively simple. The fundamental idea is to try to present each topic or subject in its intellectual and historical context. In practice, this means that we have attempted to develop a model of a retrieval system that recognizes the truth of Matthew Lipman's (1991, p. 17) observation that "disciplines are only trivially the information they contain; more important, they are the structures of relationships into which such information is organized." In the next section, we demonstrate how an information retrieval system might be designed that would actually help people learn about a relatively complex topic: strategic planning.

Obviously, there are many ways in which we could structure strategic planning. Historically, this multiplicity of ways of viewing a subject has posed serious problems for our paper-based systems. However, if we develop our strategic planning schemas using hypertext, we can develop and display multiple perspectives on the field of management theory. Once the client has told the system to search for subjects in context (and not a keyword subject search), the initial screen would show the major alternatives, thus allowing the client to select the perspective that seems the best match. If we assume that the client wanted to search for information about strategic planning, the customer would select the strategic planning category selection.

In a real system, a diagram showing between seven and ten major topics would appear on the screen. By selecting any of these topics, we could call up the next level of detail to demonstrate how we would use hypertext links to drill down to more specific topics. If we wanted information about the different strategic schools, we could click on the link "Strategic Schools." (For example, we could use Mintzberg, Ahlstrand, and Lampel's (1998) taxonomy, which includes the following schools:

- Rational School
- Environmental School
- Entrepreneurial School
- Political School
- Rational School
- Learning School

At each diagram level, a brief literature review would be provided that would explain the basics ideas and concepts. In many respects the quality of the literature reviews will be the most critical element in success of the success of this retrieval tool. Each of the essays would contain recommendations for further study. The recommended texts would be arranged by subtopic; and a summary of the contents of each document would be included. Furthermore, a brief review of the importance of the book and its role in the discipline literature would be furnished.

At this second level, the readings and the explanatory essay would discuss the basics of each school and their importance. For specific details about the rational strategic school, the client would click on the box labeled "Rational School." Once again, the client would be able to view a selection of relevant documents that have been annotated by an expert in the field. Best of all, the structure of the discipline would be made explicit in the intelligent in the intelligent knowledge-base's diagrams of the discipline's key ideas and their interconnections.

Mintzberg, Ahlstrand, and Lampel's strategic schools are only one of many possible representations. For instance, van der Heijden classifies strategic schools into three categories: rationalists, evolutionists, and processualists (1996, pp. 31–36). As such, van der Heijden's classification is an equally valid way of looking at strategic planning.

Of course, the real issue is not to determine which perspective is the "correct" one. Since none of these perspectives on strategic management is the "correct" one, the real concern is to develop an information system that can show multiple perspectives of such complex subjects. With hypertext, imagination, and a lot of hard work, we have the tools needed to show multiple overviews of strategic planning (or any other complex field.) Using the same tools, we can also show the interrelationships among the various schools of strategic thought. For example, in a true hypertext system the client would have the opportunity to compare the attributes and characteristics of each of the strategic planning schools by viewing each school of thought in detail. Such an approach would allow a student to focus on the primary attributes of, for instance, the rationalist and the learning schools. If the client were interested in the premises that underlie the rationalist school, for example, the screen would show the client the diagram that contained the premises, historical antecedents, and major assumptions of the rationalist school. By drilling down, the client would be able to see the information and sources that described, in detail, each premise, such as the following: 1) CEO drives process; 2) the process is rational; 3) the model must be simple; 4) strategy is based on an analysis of the organization's strengths and weaknesses.

At each of the these lower levels, the client would be able to see the most authoritative and recognized texts on the subject. In addition, a brief essay would describe the key issues and topics and suggest books, articles, and Web sites for further research. The essay would also contain links to other relevant and related topics so that the client would be able to navigate through the main ideas of each topic.

Although this simple narrative description cannot capture the multiple interrelationships of a truly graphics-based system, it does give at least some idea of how an intelligent knowledge base could use hypertext to create a rich learning environment that would deliver information customized to meet the client's individual needs.

AID TO REFLECTIVE THINKING

> Every person seems to have a limited capacity to assimilate information, and if it is presented to him too rapidly and without adequate repetition, this capacity will break down.
> —R. Duncan Luce, *Developments in Mathematical Psychology*

Another great advantage of this model is that it would allow the client to select the level of detail desired. A novice would naturally enter the upper levels of the discipline that would contain the works that provide a more general overview. By drilling down in the specific subdisciplines, the customer could retrieve more specific and specialized information. In addition, the retrieval system would also be designed with a weighting factor that the searcher could use to limit recall to the most relevant 5 percent or the top 10 percent, or even all of the documents. In any case, the searcher would have a powerful tool that would avoid the common problem faced by library users who do a subject search and retrieve either hundreds of documents or none. Of course, the retrieval system would also support the standard queries available in intelligent databases, including query by example.

By allowing people to make links between documents written at different levels, the students would be able to read at a comfortable level. It would also allow, according to Drexler (1986, p. 226), readers to peek at parallel discussions that dig a bit deeper. By allowing people to make links between similar presentations written at different levels, the system would assist students in improving the depth of their understanding. To further enhance their learning, the software would be designed to provide links to primers and basic definitions, which would allow readers to "pause for review—instantly, privately, and without embarrassment" (p. 226). For the more advanced student, the retrieval system would allow the reader to track the main ideas while perusing they peruse the arguments supporting or criticizing an idea. Most important of all, the arguments would be displayed in context as a network of interconnected ideas. While "readers still won't be able to judge ideas instantly or perfectly . . . they will be able to judge them faster and better. . . . In this way," Drexler claims, "hypertext will help us with a great task of our time: judging what lies ahead, and adjusting our thinking to prospects that shake the foundations of established worldviews. Hypertext will strengthen our foresight" (p. 225).

Two other significant advantages that this system would offer are the ability to present the information in multiple perspectives and the ability to display interdisciplinary materials. By its very nature, hypertext offers an almost effortless means of showing multiple interrelationships among records. Using hypertext documents allows us to "recognize links and similarities between pieces of information that are normally stored in separate locations." Without hypertext we would not be able to show the "rich network of cause and effect relationships" (Parsaye et al., 1989, p. 223). In the proposed system, hypertext would allow us to display documents from several perspectives. For instance, Mintzberg et al.'s (1998) *Strategic Safari* might be displayed to a client who was searching for books on strategic planning in learning organizations. Another client, whose interest is in the theory of business decision making, would retrieve the book because of its discussion of logical incrementalism.

Another, perhaps more telling, example is C. West Churchman's (1971) famous systems text, *The Design of Inquiring Systems*. As the name implies, this book is about systems theory. However, the book could just as easily be considered as a text on applied epistemology. In any case, thanks to hypertext's ability to link documents, we now have the ability to locate interdisciplinary documents and actually view them from multiple perspectives.

Hypertext's ability to display interdisciplinary information is particularly critical today. First, with approximately 10,000 specialties, our knowledge-base has become quite fragmented (Hamming, 1997, p. 73). Second, the emphasis on systems thinking and systems solutions makes it doubly important that our retrieval systems find a way to knit together the patches of knowledge that have been scattered among the thousands of disciplines. Since both the problems and solutions to many of our most intractable problems—poverty, pollution, crime, illiteracy, and health costs—encompass multiple disciplines, the traditional method of categorizing and classifying knowledge into discrete packets works as an artificial barrier that makes the problems even more intractable because key pieces of information are scattered across so many disciplines. The noted scientist and philosopher Edward O. Wilson (1998, p. 8) observes that:

> The greatest enterprise of the mind has always been and always will be the attempted linkage of the sciences and humanities. The ongoing fragmentation of knowledge and resulting chaos in philosophy are not reflections of the real world but artifacts of scholarship.

Wilson (1998, p. 9) notes that the interconnections among environmental policy, ethics, social science, and biology illustrate how interdependent knowledge is:

> We already think of these four domains as closely connected, so that rational inquiry in one informs reasoning in the other three. Yet undeniably each stands apart in the contemporary academic mind. Each has its own practitioners, language, modes of analysis, and standards of validation. The result is confusion, and confusion was correctly identified by Francis Bacon four centuries ago as the most fatal of errors, which occurs wherever argument or inference passes from one world of experience to another.

THE IMPORTANCE OF KNOWLEDGE MANAGEMENT FOR LIBRARIES

> Indeed, the new source of wealth is not material, it is information, knowledge applied to work to create value.
> —Walter Wriston

In this new era, wealth is the product of knowledge. Knowledge and information—
not just scientific knowledge, but news, advice, entertainment, communications,
service—have become the economy's primary raw materials and its most
important products.
—Thomas A. Stewart (1997)

It is the rate at which individuals learn that determines an organization's
sustainable competitive advantage. If a smart organization is to be qualitatively
different from and better than traditional organizations, discovery and action
cannot be limited to a few senior managers.
—Michael E. McGill and John W. Slocum, Jr.

Although we are constantly bombarded with pronouncements that the information age is going to revolutionize society, it is only when we look at individual examples from business that we can see how profoundly information technology has already rewritten the competitive rules. Stewart (1997, p. ix) summarizes the changes in the following passage:

> Knowledge is more valuable and more powerful than natural resources, big factories, or fat bankrolls. In industry after industry, success comes to the companies that have the best information or wield it most effectively—not necessarily the companies with the most muscle. Wal-Mart, Microsoft, and Toyota didn't become great companies because they were richer than Sears, IBM, and General Motors—on the contrary. But they had something far more valuable than physical or financial assets. They had intellectual capital.

Since the early 1990s, business thinkers have elevated learning into the prime strategic directive. There was almost unanimous agreement that learning is the only source of a sustainable competitive advantage (McGill & Slocum, 1994, p. 13; see also Davenport & Prusak, 1998; Martin, 1995; O'Dell, Grayson, & Essaides, 1998; and Ulrich et al., 1993). The successful corporations were no longer the largest or most efficient. Rather, "the most successful corporations are those that learn in every way possible and put what is learned to the best use," writes Martin (1995, p. 4). "Knowledge," he continues, "constantly renewed and enhanced, is the primary source of competitive advantage." Amidon takes the next step and proclaims that "the new source of wealth is knowledge, not labor, land, or financial capital. It is the intangible, intellectual assets that must be managed" (1997, p. 17). And if learning and knowledge are the keys to competitive success, then the ultimate, sustainable competitive advantage is "the ability to learn faster than the competitors" (De Geus, 1988, p. 71).

CRITICAL SKILLS OF THE KNOWLEDGE WORKER: IMPLICATIONS FOR LIBRARIES

> We win because we hire the smartest people. We improve products based on feedback, until they're the best. We have retreats each year where we think about where the world is heading.
> —Bill Gates (1997), *Time*

Given the newfound importance of learning and knowledge management, it naturally follows that the desired skills in the labor force have also changed. Crawford (1991, p. 126) observes that the critical skill needed by workers in the knowledge economy "is the ability to think—to synthesize, make generalizations, divide into categories, draw inferences, distinguish between fact and opinion, and organize facts to analyze a problem." Robert Reich (1991, p. 229) states that the capacity "for discovering patterns and meanings" is the very essence of the new level of skills that will be needed in coming years. In short, the successful employee "will be doing what robots can't do, which means their work will call for the exercise of sophisticated intelligence" (Caine & Caine, 1994, p. 15). We no longer require individuals with the skills needed to work on an assembly line; rather, we need individuals who have the skills needed to be problem solvers, decisionmakers, and adept negotiators.

In the information age, professional education no longer centers around memorizing facts and procedures but upon acquiring general problem-solving skills and the creative ability to manipulate ideas. In a real sense, a solid theoretical understanding of a discipline provides the essential framework needed to support a lifetime of professional learning. In other words, education in the postindustrial era will have to "concentrate more on development of those skills that are poorly done by computers. Development of creativity and holistic thinking ability should have top priority" (Blakeslee, 1983, p. 113).

Given the needs of business and educational institutions and their long-term importance to libraries, it makes sense that libraries would strive to develop information systems that were optimized to support the needs of the knowledge worker. In particular, the development of intelligent knowledge-bases would have great appeal for the adult learner who is attempting to learn new skills. Clearly, intelligent knowledge-bases would have considerable appeal to large segments of society as both an information retrieval systems and a learning tool.

COMPETING IN THE INFORMATION AGE

> The most profound technologies are those that disappear. They weave themselves into the fabric of everyday life until they are indistinguishable from it.
> —Mark Weiser, *Xerox Corporation*

Although it is difficult to pick up a magazine or listen to a news program without being reminded that this is the information age, there is surprisingly little discussion of the underlying technologies and economic forces that drive the information revolution. Recently, however, there has been a growing emphasis on understanding how information technology has redefined the ways in which our organizations function and compete. An understanding of the new competitive rules for the digital age begins with the two most famous laws of the computer age: Moore's Law and Metcalfe's Law.

Moore's Law, named after the cofounder of Intel, Gordon Moore, states that the power and performance of computer chips will double every 18 to 24 months (Dertouzos, 1997, p. 321). As a result of nearly four decades of exponential growth, computers have become so cheap and so powerful that they are found in nearly every product. The demand for computing power has become so insatiable that computer chips are now being produced at a rate of nearly a billion chips per minute (Oliver, 1999, p. 5). And during the past 20 years, computer hardware has undergone a 100,000-fold improvement in price and performance (Moschella, 1997, p. v).

Metcalfe's Law, named after Bob Metcalfe, the inventor of Ethernet and founder of 3Com, states that the cost of expanding a network tends to increase linearly as additional nodes are added; however, the value of the network increases as the square of the number of its users (Downes and Mui, 1998, p. 5; Moschella, 1997, p. 101).

Since the early 1990s, the combined effect of these two laws has transformed society in a remarkable number of ways. The constant doubling of price and performance predicted by Moore's Law has made computing power so cheap that it has transformed nearly every item from toasters to automobiles. Given the importance and ubiquity of computers, the need to share data across computer systems became a high priority for information technology managers. When the Internet's communication protocols reached critical mass sometime in 1993, it became the de facto communications standard of the world (Downes & Mui, 1998, pp. 6–7). Subsequently the value of each additional node and user became so great that the Internet exerted an enormous gravitational force that sucked in every device, network, and marketing expert in its path. Now that the inexpensive global computing network is in place, Moore's Law and Metcalfe's Law have begun to operate like an enormous feedback loop—constantly reinforcing each other.

In many respects the Internet is a classic example of network economics and Metcalfe's Law. As more people connect to the Internet, the benefits of being connected to the Internet become greater. Since the advantages to being on the Internet increase constantly, more people and more organizations join each month, which causes the importance of the Internet to continue spiraling upward at an exponential rate. For business firms, the Internet has already become the marketing tool of the future (Sterne, 1999, p. 33).

The market today is improving its efficiency at the speed of Moore's and Metcalfe's Laws. Traditional industries, whose aging and expensive technology infrastructure keeps them from changing at anywhere near the pace of the market itself, find it increasingly difficult to compete in the digital marketplace. This adoption gap has been described by Downes & Mui (1999, p. 7) as the Law of Diminishing Firms. As the market becomes more efficient, the size and organizational complexity of the modern industrial firm becomes uneconomic. The current trends toward downsizing and outsourcing are simply the early indicators that the digital revolution has changed the rules of competition. The "networked firm" and the "boundaryless organization" are simply two terms to describe the new firm that is built on complicated webs of well-managed relationships.

TRANSACTION COSTS

> It's the oldest lesson in the world: Unless you're customer driven, you go out of business.
> —Walter Wriston

> The sure path to oblivion is to stay exactly where you are.
> —Bernard Fauber

Markets are becoming more efficient because the computer and the Internet have combined to reduce the transaction costs involved in the selling and distribution of goods and services. Traditionally firms and individuals tended to buy their products locally because of transaction costs. For example, let us assume that a bookstore in Seattle, Washington, named Amazon.com is selling the latest bestseller for 30 percent off. Since the book retails for $30.00, we can save $9.00 by buying it from Amazon.com. Because we live in Florida, the costs of driving to Seattle (the transaction costs) far outweigh the $9.00 saving, so it makes much more sense for us to buy the book at the retail price from our local bookstore. With the Internet and cheap computing power, however, the transaction costs for many purchases have fallen to zero or nearly zero in the digital marketplace. As a result, it now makes it cheaper for us to buy the discounted book from a vendor in Seattle than from a bookstore in Miami. In effect, the reduction in transaction costs means that there are no more local markets in the age of the Internet. It is no wonder that the senior editor of *The Economist*, Frances Cairncross (1997, p. 1), believes that "the death of distance as a determinant of the cost of communicating will probably be the single most important force shaping society in the first half of the next century."

In addition to transaction costs, online vendors also have several competitive advantages because they are in a network environment. First, they do not have to build costly outlets to reach their target customers. Hagel and Armstrong (1997, p. 12) estimate that the cost of buying and maintaining physical assets translates into a 30 to 40 percent cost advantage for the networked organization. In addition to lower fixed costs, the networked vendor also has a broader geographic reach. Networked vendors have the ability to capture more information from the customer. In practice, this means that they will often be able to deal directly with their end customers, without the assistance of traditional intermediaries such as wholesalers, retailers, and distributors.

THE DIGITAL ECONOMY AND THE RISE OF NETWORKS

One could reasonably expect the chairman of AT&T to know what his corporation will be in ten years from now. He doesn't. One could, within reason, expect the chairman of AT&T to be able to predict how technology will transform his business a decade hence. He can't. At the least, he should know who his major competitors will be in 2005. Stumped again. But here is what he does know: something startling, intriguing, and profound is afoot.
—Robert Allen

The fundamental reason that civilization is limited by information is quite simple: Civilization *is* information. Most of the factors that characterize a civilization—its ethics and laws, its technology, its philosophy and religion, its literature and art— are forms of information. And civilizations are generally limited more by lack of information than by lack of physical resources.
—Douglas S. Robertson (1998)

The new economy, created by shrinking computers and expanding communications, "represents a tectonic upheaval in our commonwealth, a far more turbulent reordering than mere digital hardware has produced" (Kelly, 1998, p. 1). The new economy has three distinguishing characteristics: It is global; it derives its greatest value from sale and exchange of ideas and information; and it is intensely interlinked. Kelly (pp. 1–2) continues:

The new economic order has its own distinct opportunities and pitfalls. If past economic transformations are any guide, those who play by the new rules will prosper, while those who ignore them will not. We have seen only the beginnings of the anxiety, loss, excitement, and gains that many people will experience as our world shifts to a new highly technical planetary economy.

To remain competitive, we need to understand how networks and computers have changed the rules of competition. We need, in short, to understand the marketplace's "digital rules." As Tapscott (1996, p. xv) notes, the age of networked intelligence is a time of peril. When individuals, organizations, or societies fall behind or fail to understand the new digital rules, punishment will be swift. Communication, according to Kelly (1998, p. 5), is the foundation of society, of our culture, of our humanity, of our own individual identity, and of all economic systems. This is why networks are such a big deal. Communication is so close to culture and society itself that the effects of technologizing it are beyond the scale of a mere industrial-sector cycle. Communication, and its ally computers, is a special case in economic history. Not because it happens to be the fashionable leading business sector of our day, but because its cultural, technological, and conceptual impacts reverberate at the root of our lives.

In *The New Renaissance*, Robertson (1998, pp. 8–9) makes a persuasive case that the computer revolution will have an effect on society as great as those three other great information innovations: language, writing, and printing. Robertson (p. 7) contends that:

> History has never seen a revolution on the scale of the one that is being triggered by computer technology. The closest historical parallels, the revolutions of the Renaissance, occurred on a far smaller scale than the ones being touched off today by computer technology.

Although still in its infancy, the information revolution has already begun to transform the rules of competition in virtually every industry. "We are just beginning the radical rethinking of the way businesses, schools, libraries, and governments are seen as contributing value to society" write Edvinsson and Malone (1997, p. 22). They note that we have two choices: to be in "the vanguard of this movement, better prepared and more experienced than your competitors. Or wait, until it washes over you and tosses you forward struggling to keep from being dashed and drowned."

INFORMATION RULES

The new economy is an based on innovation. Beginning with their first orientation
Microsoft employees are constantly told that they must make their own products
obsolete. If you've just developed a great product, your goal is to develop a better
one that will make the first one obsolete. If you don't make it obsolete, someone
else will.
—Don Tapscott (1996)

Again, it is a condition of modernity that at any given moment just about everyone
is mostly out of date, even on matters that truly concern them.
—Derek Leebaert, *The Future of Software*

As many companies have already discovered, the rules for competing in a networked environment are very different from those of a traditional business. In fact, Martin (1999, p. 11) claims that the logic of networked enterprises is often the exact opposite of what we would expect. Surviving in the networked future will involve understanding how computers and networks have redefined the marketplace and the rules of competition. Although much remains uncertain, it is already possible to identify some common themes. The following guidelines are loosely based, in part, on the writings of Davis and Meyer, 1998; Downes and Mui, 1997; Kelly, 1998, and Martin, 1999:

- Networking makes decentralized control a competitive advantage;
- Networking fosters global competition by lowering transaction costs;
- The theory of diminishing returns does not apply to information networks because of Metcalfe's Law;
- The cost of sharing digital information is minimal because networks allow unlimited sharing;
- Access to materials depends on network access, not physical proximity;
- The key future technologies for the digital library are those that enhance and amplify intellectual collaboration;
- The key to future success is to develop new products that add value for the client, not in improving the efficiency of internal procedures;
- Speed and fast reaction time must be part of the library community's culture;
- Libraries must network with businesses, communities, universities, museums, and clients;
- The future is in developing intangibles (information, software, relationships, and customized services), not physical plant;
- Librarians must involve the customer in the development of new products and services;
- The client must be allowed to add value to the network by creating online communities and discussion forums;
- The library must offer customized and individualized service to each client;
- Managing knowledge will be the library's raison d'être;
- Library strategy must be based on maximizing the value of the network, not the value of the individual library; and
- Because change is the norm in the information age, the most effective long-term strategy is innovation.

THE MASTER RULE: SOFTWARE REIGNS

> In the end, the location of the economy is not in the technology, be it the microchip or the global telecommunications network. It is in the human mind.
> —Alan Webber, *Harvard Business Review*

> No matter how good your product, you are only 18 months away from failure.
> —Nathan Myhrvold, *The Road Ahead* (with Bill Gates)

The final, and most important rule of all is: All of the rules are subject to change without notice. This final rule poses serious problems for the library community because it has traditionally viewed itself as the preserver of our intellectual heritage. Like all organizations focused on protecting our heritage, libraries have been intensely conservative. However, as we have seen, the rules for survival have changed. Like all institutions that are part of the information industry, libraries now operate according to the rules of software. In a very real sense, software has become the library because the software now determines what the client sees, what the client accesses, and what the library looks like to the client. Even more important, software now determines the type and quality of services that the library can provide as well as the future services that the library might offer. As a result, it is difficult to disagree with Quinn, Jordan, and Zien's (1997, p. 4) claim that software has become the key driving force of our economy:

> Software is radically changing every element in innovation, from basic research, to needs analysis in the marketplace, to design of virtually all products and services, to model building and prototyping, through initial and mass production, to distribution, marketing, and post-sale service. It enables innovators to work together in new modes: in virtual laboratories, virtual skunk works, remote independent collaborations, and tightly integrated worldwide experimentation and production to simultaneously achieve greatest intellectual advance, highest quality, greatest flexibility, and lowest cost. Its software systems are now an integral part of any enterprise's organization, culture, and innovation–value creation system.

Software has become the critical competitive weapon in the age of networks because "software alone enables zero marginal costs, mass customization, the processing and management of mass communications, and the underlying potential for industry-wide transformation." (Papows, 1998, p. 57). Software's greatest power, however, lies in its ability to enhance our intellect; software has become "the key factor in developing, leveraging, and diffusing all levels of intellect" (Quinn et al., 1997, p. 2). Libraries are now in the software business because software is how we add value for our customers. Library professionals must now recognize that computers and networking have profoundly redefined their venerable institutions. This realization will not come quickly or easily; as Edvinsson and Malone (1997, p. 21) note:

> It is human nature to assume that any important new innovation will simply improve upon what preceded it . . . and then to be stunned when it breaks out into new territory of its own. Thus, the march of computers through corporations has been one long story of users trying to confine it to improving existing processes—bookkeeping, manufacturing, management reporting, payroll, sales—only to find that it leads to a radical restructuring of the entire discipline.

BUILDING ONLINE COMMUNITIES

> In an age where increasingly all our social problems seem intractable,
> "new thinking" has become a catch-phrase. Unfortunately, most who propose it
> stop with the label.
> —Ian Mitroff and Harold Linstone

Perhaps the greatest advantage offered by intelligent knowledge-bases is the ability to furnish information anywhere, anytime, and in any format. Since our knowledge-bases will use the Internet as a distribution channel, the network will truly have a global reach. Even more important, we can leverage the information retrieval capabilities of our new retrieval systems by encouraging our customers to share their insights and thinking by developing online communities. To date libraries have been slow to embrace the idea of developing online communities. Of course, in this regard the same could be said of most commercial enterprises, which have also "been slow to understand and make use of the unique community-building capabilities of the medium" (Armstrong & Hagel, 1998, p. 63).

In its early stages, the online communities might be little more than a few bulletin boards that would allow customers to share opinions about books or common interests. As such, the system would emulate Web practices already in widespread use, such as Amazon.com's feature that allows readers to share their opinions about individual titles. Reader comments add a valuable supplement to the standard review sources as well as establish a stronger bond with the customer.

While the ability to share opinions about books would certainly be important and valued feature, it remains a relatively primitive electronic community. There are, however, other roles for the online community that would be a natural extension of the library's traditional role as the community information manager. In the beginning the new electronic communities would serve the same kinds of social needs that library clients have traditionally enjoyed. More specifically, electronic communities based on common interests in specific topics such as investment, science-fiction novels, and mystery clubs. Of course, the common interests could also center "around certain life experiences that often are very intense and can lead to the formation of deep personal connections," such as divorce, widowhood, serious diseases, and addiction (Armstrong & Hagel, 1998, p. 65). In most cases these different interest groups would typically share information about common issues as well as information about finding additional information.

For most business writers, online communities have a strong appeal because they are seen as a powerful marketing tool. Armstrong and Hagel (1998, pp. 63–64) argue that

> commercial success in the on-line area will belong to those businesses that organize electronic communities to meet multiple social and commercial needs. By creating strong on-line communities, businesses will be able to build customer loyalty to a

degree that today's marketers can only dream of and, in turn, generate strong economic returns.

Online communities represent much more than a marketing opportunity for libraries. They also offer libraries an opportunity to expand upon their traditional role as an information provider. With a minimal investment in technology, libraries can now sponsor online forums that will discuss important issues on both the local and national level. Potentially, these online forums could also function as learning networks that would allow the participants to exchange ideas and information freely (Amidon, 1997, p. 24). Pinchot and Pinchot (1993, p. 278) believe that such networks can actually promote faster learning as well as stimulate pluralism and a hunger for new ideas. Best of all, such networks would be an effective way to get a larger segment of the population involved in learning.

COLLECTIVE INTELLIGENCE: THE NEW SOCRATIC DIALOG

Human history becomes more and more a race between education and catastrophe.
—H. G. Wells, *The Outline of History*

Computers are useless. They can only give you answers.
—Pablo Picasso

Knowledge is the only instrument of production that is not subject to diminishing returns.
—J. M. Clark

One of the recurrent problems faced by our increasingly complex society is our inability to make intelligent decisions about complicated problems. In fact, the problems facing the electorate are often so complicated that most people lack the knowledge to make decisions about the economy, the environment, or the use of technology (Drexler 1986, pp. 203–204).

It is difficult to disagree with Drexler's (p. 205) claim that "our greatest problem is how we handle problems." The current debates over nuclear power, coal, chemical wastes, low-level radiation, and the environment are precursors to debates over even more complex problems (genetic engineering and "anti-aging" drugs are only the most obvious). All too often these complex problems are dealt with in either a 15-second sound bite or by partisan wrangling. In the ensuing welter of claims and counterclaims, the cautious statements by scrupulous scientists make little impression in the public debate. In such a setting, the "debates become sharp and angry, divisions grow, and the smoke of battle obscures the facts. Paralysis or folly often follows," concludes Drexler (p. 205).

What is needed is a new arena that will support learning and investigation, that will provide a forum for debate based on facts. A logical site for such forums would be the online communities developed by libraries. Since the libraries would offer a neutral site, plus access to intelligent knowledge-bases, the participants would have access to information and hard facts that would inform, not inundate. Such a site would offer an ideal battleground where conflicting ideas could be pitted against one another. If the sites follow Drexler's (1986, pp. 207–208) suggestion and adopt the rules and procedures followed by refereed journals, the battle of ideas could take place in a reasonably fair and orderly environment. While it is true that refereed journals occasionally fail to present the issues fairly, they are still the best process that our society has developed for carrying on critical discussions.

Unlike journals, which are too slow and serve academic interests, the library's online communities would have the speed needed to carry on a public debate. Intelligent knowledge-bases would provide an information-rich environment in which each side could then discuss the issues. Drexler recommends that the fact forum begin with a summary of the facts. Each side would then begin the debate by listing the facts, in order of importance. The online discussion would then begin with the statements from each side's list (Drexler, 1986, p. 209). In the following rounds, a referee would supervise the cross-examination and rebuttals. A panel of experts would then write an opinion about any of the issues that remain contested and publish the opinion on the site. The output of the fact forum would be the background arguments, statements of agreement and expert opinion (p. 209). Although Drexler's fact forum will not solve all of society's problems, it promises to be a much better method of conducting public debate than the current system, for, as he (p. 213) wisely observes:

> No institution will be able to eliminate corruption and error, but fact forums will be guided, however imperfectly, by an improved standard for the conduct of public debate; they will have to fall a long way before becoming worse than the system we have today.

To achieve this vision of the library as an powerful tool for learning is beyond the resources of any individual library. The library community, as a whole, will have to combine their resources if they want to succeed in building a library capable of meeting the needs of the information age. Even in its relatively brief history, the Internet has demonstrated the power and appeal of being able to access any information, anytime, anyplace, and in any format. Equally obvious, the library community will have to establish partnerships with the publishing industry and academic experts to realize the dream of creating the intelligent knowledge-base. Fortunately, libraries have had a long and successful history collaborating with the publishing industry and with educational institutions. It is not too much to hope that they will be able translate this vision into what will become the modern equivalent of the Alexandrian Library.

THE NEW ALEXANDRIAN LIBRARY

The best way to create the future is to invent it.
—Alan Kay, Apple Computer

That which has always been accepted by everyone, everywhere, is almost certain
to be false.
—Paul Valéry, *Tel Quel*

The traumatic transition from an industrial to a knowledge society affects
everything from schools to nation states, from the production of wealth to the
organizations that produce it.
—Walter Wriston

The Alexandrian Library, according to legend, owed its existence to Alexander
the Great, who "had imagined a great library in his namesake city" (Boorstin,
1992, p. 48). The Ptolemies translated his vision into reality when the royal
library became the first repository of the West's literary inheritance (Harris,
1995). For the next 600 years, Alexandria reigned as the intellectual center of
the Mediterranean, "thanks to the great Library and Museion . . ." (Burke, 1978,
p. 18). The Library was literally the treasure-house of the ancient world. Its
nearly half a million manuscripts contained "virtually all that was then known"
(Burke, 1978, p. 18).

Although it is not known exactly when the great library burned, its destruction
has not prevented the Alexandrian Library from remaining a potent symbol for
librarians and scholars. The grand vision of all human knowledge collected into
one, easily accessed location continues to fire our imaginations. In some respects
the Alexandrian Library has, like the Holy Grail, inspired us with its very
unattainability. With the advent of printing, the possibility of collecting all
knowledge in one great library became less and less feasible as the printing presses
inexorably increased their yearly output.

Paradoxically, in a period when the continued existence of libraries is openly
questioned, the library profession has at long last acquired the tools needed to create
a new Alexandrian library that would, like its fabled ancestor, serve as the repository
of virtually all human knowledge. Even more impressive, we also have the technology needed to access the vast amounts of information that the new Alexandrian
library would house. What we do not have is the commitment and organizational
structure needed to transform our dreams into a new vision of the library that is not
defined by bricks and mortar. Most of all, we have yet to realize that storing
information is not enough; we need to reclaim our position as society's knowledge
manager and learning forum.

Before we can translate this vision into reality, we need to need to answer some
very practical questions, such as:

- How do we want the vision of the library to change in the next five to 10 years?
- What must we do to make sure that the library evolves in a way that adds value for the customer?
- What skills and capabilities must we begin to acquire in order to survive in a digital world?
- How can we change from being a repository of information into an organization that manages information?
- How do we make the intellectual shift required to change from managing a physical library to developing a digital library?
- And most of all, how can we transform our institution so that it becomes a tool for learning and debate?

There is nothing magical about these questions. The list is certainly incomplete, but it is a start. In today's environment we are no longer playing by the traditional rules that served libraries so well for the past 500 years. Instead, the game is now played by digital rules, which means that constant and rapid change continually rewrite the correct answers. We live in a time when ". . . success is the reward for asking the right questions" and "failure is the result of thinking you have all the answers" (Dunham et al., 1993, p. xxii). At a minimum the successful library must be able to: 1) know how to transfer and leverage knowledge and best practices; 2) turn knowledge into competitive advantage by getting closer to the customer and by adding value for the customer; and 3) know how to translate learning into change so that the learning is reflected in the changes to the organization's infrastructure, culture, technology, and processes (O'Dell et al., 1998, p. xii).

Although there is much about the future that is uncertain, we can safely assume that we will never be able to permanently fix things or derive a final answer for our institution's problems. In the long run, our only hope is to develop an organization that can learn and respond to new demands. As a result, we want to acknowledge that we do not have all the answers—we do not even have all of the questions. However, we also believe that the best guarantor of the future is for the library to build on its traditional skills and vision by becoming society's information manager. By becoming a tool that helps people learn, the library will have taken a major step to reclaiming its position as a valuable and valued institution. At the same time, we also admit that change will invalidate many of the details of the vision of the library as a learning tool. T. S. Eliot said it best in "Little Gidding":

> We shall not cease from exploration
> And the end of all our exploring
> Will be to arrive where we started
> And know the place for the first time.

THE NEW PROFESSIONALS

It is the first step in sociological wisdom, to recognize that the major advances in
civilization are processes which all but wreck the societies in which they
occur—like unto an arrow in the hand of a child. The art of free society consists
first in the maintenance of the symbolic code; and secondly in fearlessness of
revision, to secure that the code serves those purposes which satisfy an enlightened
reason. Those societies which cannot combine reverence to their symbols with
freedom of revision, must ultimately decay either from anarchy, or from the slow
atrophy of a life stifled by useless shadows.
—Alfred North Whitehead, *Symbolism, Its Meaning and Effect*

This time, like all other times, is a very good one, if we but know what to do with it.
—Ralph Waldo Emerson

At the end of this long journey, we turn, once again, to the man whose vision and
imagination continues to drive the library profession: Vannevar Bush. We hope that
many librarians are ready to become members of Bush's (1945, p. 108) new
"profession of trail blazers" and that among "those who find delight in the task of
establishing useful trails through the enormous mass of the common record" there
will be many librarians among their number. To paraphrase Abraham Lincoln, the
library profession "can't escape the responsibility of tomorrow by evading it today."
The digital era has arrived, and we can either capitalize on its promise or become
a historical relic. To survive, we must heed Thomas J. Watson's warning (cited in
Pugh, 1995, p.322): "There is no business in the world which can hope to move
forward if it does not keep abreast of the times, look into the future and study the
probable demands of the future."

References

Ackoff, R. L. (1981). *Creating the corporate future: Plan or be planned for*. New York: Wiley.

Adams, J. A. (1988). The computer catalog: A democratic or authoritarian technology? *Library Journal, 113*, 31–36.

Albrecht, K. (1992). *The only thing that matters: Bringing the power of the customer into the center of your business*. New York: Harper Business.

Allen, C., Kania, D., & Yaeckel, B. (1998). *Internet world guide to one-to-one Web marketing*. New York: Wiley.

Altman, E. (1979). Editorial, *Library Research, 1* (Winter 1979), 293–294.

Amidon, D. M. (1997). *Innovation strategy for the knowledge economy: The Ken awakening*. Boston: Butterworth-Heinemann.

Archer, M. (1990). Theory, culture, and post-industrial society. In M. Featherstone (Ed.), *Global culture: Nationalism, globalization and modernity* (pp. 97–120). London: Sage.

Argyris, C., & Schön, D. (1978). *Organizational learning: A theory of action perspective*. Reading, MA: Addison-Wesley.

Armstrong, A., & Hagel, J., III (1998). The real value of on-line communities. In D. A. Klein (Ed.), *The strategic management of intellectual capital* (pp. 63–71). Woburn, MA: Butterworth-Heinemann.

Ansoff, H. I. (1988). *The new corporate strategy*. New York: Wiley.

Atkinson, R. (1993). The coming contest. *College & Research Libraries,* 458–460.

Ayre, R. (1994). Making the Internet connection. *PC Magazine, 13,* 118–135.

Bacon, K. H. (1990, February 23). Scrolling through libraries of the future. *Wall Street Journal*, p. B3.

Band, W. A. (1991). *Creating value for customers: Designing and implementing a total corporate strategy*. New York: Wiley.

Barker, J. A. (1992). *Paradigms: The business of discovering the future*. New York: Harper Business.

Barnes, B. (1982). *T. S. Kuhn and social science*. New York: Columbia University Press.

Baron, J. (1994). *Thinking and deciding*. (2nd ed.). New York: Cambridge University Press.

Bates, M. J. (1986, November). Subject access in online catalogs: A decision model. *Journal of the American Society for Information Science, 37,* 357–376.

Battin, P. (1986, April). The library: Centre of the restructured university. *Scholarly Publishing.*

Bayne, K.. (1997). *The Internet marketing plan: A practical handbook for creating, implementing and assessing your online presence.* New York: Wiley.

Bechtel, J. (1986). Conversion: A new paradigm for librarianship. *College and Research Libraries, 47,* 219–220.

Belasco, J. A. (1991). *Teaching the elephant to dance: The manager's guide to empowering change.* New York: Plume.

Belkin, N. J., & Vickery, A. (1985). *Interaction in information systems: A review of research from document retrieval to knowledge-based systems.* The British Library Board.

Bell, D. (1973). *The coming of post-industrial society.* New York: Basic Books.

Bell, D. (1980). The social framework of the information society. In T. Forester (Ed.), *The microelectronics revolution: The complete guide to the new technology and its impact on society* (pp. 500–549). Cambridge, MA: MIT Press.

Beniger, J. (1986). *The control revolution: Technological and economic origins of the information society.* Cambridge, MA: Harvard University Press.

Berninghausen, D. (1979). Intellectual freedom in librarianship: Advances and retreats. *Advances in Librarianship, 9,* 1–29.

Bigus, J. P. (1996). *Data mining with neural networks: Solving business problems from application development to decision support.* New York: McGraw-Hill.

Blair, D. C., & Maron, M. E. (1985). An evaluation of retrieval effectiveness for a full-text document retrieval system. *Communications of the ACM, 28,* 280–299.

Blakeslee, T. R. (1983). *The right brain.* New York: Berkely Books.

Bolter, J. D. (1984). *Turing's man: Western culture in the machine age.* Chapel Hill, NC: University of North Carolina Press.

Boorstin, D. J. (1992). *The creators.* New York: Random House.

Borgman, C. L. (1986). Why are online catalogs so hard to use? Lessons learned from information-retrieval studies. *Journal of American Society for Information Science, 37,* 387–400.

Boyett, J. H., & Conn, H. P. (1991). *Workplace 2000: The revolution reshaping American business.* New York: Plume.

Bradley, S. P., & Nolan, R. L. (Eds.). (1998). *Sense and respond: Capturing value in the network era.* Boston: Harvard Business School Press.

Bradshaw, J. M. (1997). An introduction to software agents. In J. M. Bradshaw (Ed.), *Intelligent agents* (pp. 3–46). Menlo Park, CA: American Association for Artificial Intelligence.

Branscomb, L. (1993). Targeting critical technologies. In L. Branscomb (Ed.), *Empowering Technology: Implementing a U.S. Strategy* (pp. 36–63). Cambridge, MA: MIT Press.

Brownstein, M. (1994). Forecast: Spinning soon. *PC Computing, 7,* 141.

Bryant, E. (1994). Reinventing the university press. *Library Journal,* 147–149.

Burke, J. (1978). *Connections.* Boston: Little, Brown and Co.

Burrus, D., & Gittines, R. (1993). *Technotrends: How to use technology to go beyond your competition.* New York: HarperBusiness.

Bush, V. (1945). As we may think. *Atlantic Monthly 176, 1* (July), 107.

Cage, M. C. (1994, September 21). The virtual library. *Chronicle of Higher Education*, pp. A23–A27.

Caine, R., & Caine, G. (1994). *Making connections: Teaching and the human brain.* Reading, MA: Addison-Wesley.

Cairncross, F. (1997). *The death of distance: How the communications revolution will change our lives.* Cambridge, MA: Harvard Business School Press.

Campbell, J. (1989). *The improbable machine: What new discoveries in artificial intelligence reveal about how the mind really works.* New York: Touchstone.

Cheong, F. (1996). *Internet agents: spiders, wanderers, brokers, and "bots."* Indianapolis, IN: New Riders.

Churchman, C. W. (1971). *The design of inquiring systems.* New York: Basic Books.

Churchman, C. W. (1979). *The systems approach* (Rev. ed.). New York: Dell.

Cleveland, H. (1991). *The knowledge executive: Leadership in an information society.* New York: E. P. Dutton.

Cleverdon, C. (1984). Optimizing convenient online access to bibliographic databases. *Information Services and Use, 4*, 37–47.

Comer, D. E. (1995). *The Internet book: Everything you need to know about computer networking and how the Internet works.* Englewood Cliffs, NJ: Prentice-Hall.

Comer, D. E. (1997). *The Internet book: Everything you need to know about computer networking and how the Internet works.* (2nd ed.). Englewood Cliffs, NJ: Prentice-Hall.

Conley, V. A. (Ed.). (1993). *Rethinking technologies.* Minneapolis, MN: University of Minnesota Press.

Conway, P. (1994, February 1). Digitizing Preservation. *Library Journal,* 42–45.

Crawford, R. (1991). *In the era of human capital.* New York: Harper Business.

Crowell, S., Caine, R. N., & Caine, G. (1998). *The re-enchantment of learning: A manual for teacher renewal and classroom transformation.* Tucson, AZ: Zephyr Press.

Davenport, T. H., & Prusak, L. (1998). *Working knowledge: How organizations manage what they know.* Boston: Harvard Business School Press.

Davidow, W. H., & Malone, M. S. (1993). *The virtual corporation: Structuring and revitalizing the corporation for the 21st century.* New York: Harper Business.

Davis, S. (1987). *Future perfect.* Reading, MA: Addison-Wesley.

Davis, S., & Davidson, B. (1991). *2020 vision.* New York: Simon & Schuster.

Davis, S., & Meyer, C. (1998). *Blur: The speed of change in the connected economy.* Reading, MA: Addison-Wesley.

De Gennaro, R. (1987). *Libraries, technology, and the information marketplace: Selected papers.* Boston: G. K. Hall.

De Geus, A. (1988, March–April). Planning and learning. *Harvard Business Review, 66,* 70–74.

Delany, P. (1993). From the scholar's library to the personal docuverse. In G. P. Landow & P. Delany (Eds.), *The digital word: Text-based computing in the humanities* (pp. 189–199). Cambridge, MA: MIT Press.

Denning, P. J., & Metcalfe, R. M. (1997). *Beyond calculation: The next fifty years of computing.*

Dertouzos, M. (1997). *What will be: How the new world of information will change our lives.* New York: HarperCollins.

Dillon, M. et al. (1993). *Assessing information on the Internet: Toward providing library services for computer-mediated communication.* Dublin, OH: OCLC Online Computer Library Center.

Ditzler, C., Early, C., & Weston, C. (1993). *The electronic information initiative phase 1: Final report.* Beltsville, MD: National Agricultural Library.

Dougherty, R. M. (1990). Needed: User-responsive research libraries. *Library Journal, 116,* 60.

Downes, L., & Mui, C. (1998). *Unleashing the killer app: Digital strategies for market dominance.* Boston: Harvard Business School Press.

Drexler, E. K. (1986). *Engines of creation.* New York: Doubleday.

Drucker, P. F. (1993). *Post-capitalist society.* New York: HarperCollins.

Dunham, A. et al. (1993). *Unique value®: The secret of all great business strategies.* New York: Macmillan.

Dyson, E. (1998, November 11). *Friction Freedom.* Forbes ASAP. [www.forbes.com/asap/98/1130/061.htm].

Edvinsson, L., & Malone, M. S. (1997). *Intellectual capital: Realizing your company's true value by finding its hidden roots.* New York: HarperCollins.

Eliot, T. S. (1963). *Collected poems, 1909–1962.* New York: Harcourt Brace.

Ellis, B. D. (1991). *Truth and objectivity (philosophical theory).* Oxford, England: Blackwell.

Emery, J. C. (1987). *Management information systems: The critical strategic resource.* Oxford, England: Oxford University Press.

Feenberg, A. (1991). *Critical theory of techology.* Oxford, England: Oxford University Press.

Foster, R. N. (1986). *Innovation: The attacker's advantage.* New York: Summit Books.

Furnas, G. W. et al. (1983). Statistical semantics: Analysis of the potential performance of keyword information systems. *Bell System Technical Journal, 62,* 1753–1806.

Furnas, G. W. et al. (1987). The vocabulary problem in human system communication. *Communications of the ACM, 30* (11), 964–971.

Gall, J. (1988). *Systemantics: The undergound text of systems lore.* Ann Arbor, MI: The General Systemantics Press.

Garrett, J. (1991). Missing Eco: On reading *The Name of the Rose* as library criticism. *Library Quarterly, 61,* 373–388.

Garvin, D. A. (1993). Building a learning organization. *Harvard Business Review, 71,* 78–91.

Gazis, D. C. (1991). Brief time, long march: The forward drive of computer technology. In *Technology 2001: The future of computing and communications.* D. Leebaet (Ed.), (pp. 41–76). Cambridge, MA: MIT Press.

Geertz, C. (1983). *Local knowledge: Further essays in interpretive anthropology.* New York: Basic Books.

Gerstein, M. S. (1987). *The technology connection: Strategy and change in the information age.* Reading, MA: Addison-Wesley.

Gerstenberger, P. G., & Allen, T. J. (1968). Criteria used by research and development engineers in the selection of an information source. *Journal of Applied Psychology, 52,* 272–279.

Gibson, C. F., & Jackson, B. B. (1987). *The information imperative: Managing the impact of information technology on businesses and people.* Lexington, MA: Lexington Books.

Gilster, P. (1997). *Digital literacy*. New York: Wiley.

Goodman, D. (1994). *Living at light speed: Your survival guide to life on the information superhighway*. New York: Random House.

Gore, A. (1994, December 8). The digital library. *Lexington Herald-Leader*, p. B24.

Grant, R. M. (1991). *Contemporary strategy analysis: Concepts, techniques, applications*. Cambridge, MA: Oxford Press.

Greene, S. L., Cannata, P. E., & Gomez, L. M. (1990). No IF's AND's or OR's: A study of database querying. *International Journal of Man Machine Systems, 32*, 303–326.

Greene, S. L., Gomez, L. M., & Devlin, S. J. (1986). A cognitive analysis of database query production. *Proceedings of the Human Factors Society*. Santa Monica, CA: 9–13.

Gregor, D., & Mandel, C. (1991, April 1). Cataloging must change! *Library Journal, 116*, 42–47.

Guillen, M. F. (1994). *Models of management: Work, authority, and organization in a comparative perspective*. Chicago: University of Chicago Press.

Hagel, J., III, & Armstrong, A. G. (1997). *Net gain: Expanding markets through virtual communities*. Boston: Harvard Business School Press.

Hamel, G., & Prahalad, C. K. (1994). *Competing for the future*. Boston: Harvard Business School Press.

Hammer, M. (1990). Reengineering work: Don't automate, obliterate. *Harvard Business Review, 68*, 104–112.

Hamming, R. W. (1997). How to think about trends. In P. J. Denning & R. M. Metcalf (Eds.), *Beyond calculation: The next fifty years of computing* (pp. 65–74). New York: Springer-Verlag.

Hammond, N. (1993). Learning with hypertext: Problems, principles and prospects. In C. McKnight, A. Dillon, & J. Richardson (Eds.), *Hypertext: A Psychological Perspective* (pp. 51–69). New York: Ellis Horwood.

Handy, C. (1989). *The age of unreason*. Boston: Harvard Business School Press.

Harris, M. H. (1995). *History of libraries in the Western world*. (4th ed.). Metuchen, NJ: Scarecrow Press.

Harris, M. H., & Hannah, S. A. (1992). Why do we study the history of libraries? A meditation on the perils of ahistoricism in the post-industrial era. *Journal of Research in Library and Information Science, 14*, 123–130.

Harris, M. H., & Hannah, S. A. (1996). "The treason of the librarians": Core communication technologies and opportunity costs in the information era. *Journal of Academic Librarianship, 22*, 3–8.

Harris, M. H., Hannah, S. A., & Harris, P. C. (1998). *Into the future: The foundations of library and information services in the post-industrial era*. (2nd ed.). Greenwich, CT: Ablex Publishing Corporation.

Harris, M. H., & Itoga, M. (1991). Becoming critical: For a theory of purpose and necessity in (Eds.), American librarianship. In C. McClure & P. Hernon, *Research in Library and Information Science*, 347–357. Norwood: Ablex.

Harris, M. H., & Tourjee, M. A. (1983). In W. Wiegand (Ed.), *Leaders in American academic librarianship: 1925–1975, William S. Dix* (pp. 50–71). Pittsburgh, PA: Beta Phi Mu.

Harter, S. P., & Jackson, S. M. (1988). Optical disc systems in libraries: Problems and issues. *RQ, 27*, 516–527.

Hazen, D. C. (1995). Collection development policies in the information age. *College and Research Libraries, 56*, 30.

Hickman, C. R., & Silva, M. A. (1984). *Creating excellence: Managing corporate culture, strategy, and change in the new age.* New York: New American Library.

Higonnet, P. (1991, August 15). Scandal on the Seine. *New York Review of Books, 38*, 32–33.

Johnson-Laird, P. N. (1988). *The computer and the mind: An introduction to cognitive science.* Cambridge, MA: Harvard University Press.

Joiner, B. L. et al. (1994). *Fourth generation management: The new business consciousness.* New York: McGraw-Hill.

Jonassen, D. H. (1993). Effects of semantically structured hypertext knowledge bases on users' knowledge structures. In C. McKnight, A. Dillon, & J. Richardson (Eds.), *Hypertext: A Psychological Perspective* (pp. 153–168). New York: Ellis Horwood.

Judson, B. (1996). *Net marketing.* New York: Wolff New Media.

Kahle, B. (1991, December 28). Access and the digital library. Usenet newsgroup, alts.

Kane, M. (1998, December 22). The year in e-commerce [Online]. Available: http://www.zdnet.com/zdnn/stories/news/0,4586,2177292,00.html.

Keen, P. G. W. (1991). *Shaping the future: Business design through information technology.* Boston: Harvard Business School Press.

Kelly, K. (1998). *New rules for the new economy: 10 radical changes for a connected world.* New York: Viking Press.

Kofman, F., & Senge, P. M. (1993). Communities of commitment: The heart of learning organizations. *Organizational Dynamics, 22*, 5–23.

Korn, L. B. (1989, May 22). How the next CEO will be different. *Fortune*, 49–52.

Kouzes, J. M., & Posner, B. Z. (1987). *The leadership challenge: How to get extraordinary things done in organizations.* San Francisco: Jossey-Bass.

Kuhn, T. S. (1970). *The structure of scientific revolutions.* (2nd ed.). Chicago: University of Chicago Press. (Original work published 1962)

Kuhn, T. S. (1977). *The essential tension: Selected studies in scientific tradition and change.* Chicago: University of Chicago Press.

Lancaster, F. W. (1968). *Information retrieval systems.* New York: Wiley.

Lancaster, F. W. (1978). Whither libraries? Or, wither libraries? *College and Research Libraries, 39*, 345–357.

Lancaster, F. W. (1991). Has technology failed us? *Information technology and library management: Festschrift in honor of Margaret Beckman.* 13th International Essen Symposium, 22–25 October 1989, ed. by Ahmed H. Helal and Joachim W. Weiss. Essen: Essen University Library.

Lancaster, F. W. (Ed.) (1995). Networked scholarly publishing. *Library Trends, 43*, whole issue.

Lancaster, F. W., Drasgow, L. S., & Marks, E. B. (1980). The role of the library in an electronic society. In F. W. Lancaster (Ed.), *The role of the library in an electronic society: Proceedings of the sixteenth annual clinic on library applications of data processing* (pp. 162–189). Urbana, IL: University of Illinois, Graduate School of Library and Information Science.

Landauer, T. K. (1995). *The trouble with computers: Usefulness, usability, and productivity.* Cambridge, MA: MIT Press.

Landauer, T. K. et al. (1993). Enhancing the usability of text through computer delivery and formative evaluation: The superbook project. In C. McKnight, A. Dillon, & J. Richardson (Eds.), *Hypertext: A psychological perspective* (pp. 71–136). New York: Ellis Horwood.

Lanham, R. A. (1993). The electronic word: Democracy, technology, and the arts. Chicago: University of Chicago Press.

Larkin, J. et al. (1980). Expert and novice performance in solving physics problems. *Science, 208*, 1342.

Lauffer, A. (1984). *Strategic marketing for not-for-profit organizations: Program and resource development.* New York: Free Press.

Lele, M. M. (1992). *Creating strategic leverage: Matching company strengths with market opportunities.* New York: Wiley.

Lemos, R. (1998, October 23). Would you curl up with an electronic book? [www.zdnet.com/zdnn/stories/news/0,4586,2154569.00.html].

Levine, J., & Baroudi, C. (1993). *The Internet for dummies.* San Mateo, CA: IDG Books Worldwide.

Levitt, T. (1986). *The marketing imagination.* New York: Free Press.

Levy, S. (1989). A spreadsheet way of knowledge. In T. Forester (Ed.), *Computers in the human context* (pp. 318–326). Cambridge, MA: MIT Press.

Lewin, K. (1948). *Resolving social conflicts.* New York: Harper & Row.

Lewis, P. H. (1990, May 13). Where the libraries are leading the way. *New York Times*, p. 8F.

Limerick, D., & Cunnington, B. (1993). *Managing the new organization: A blueprint for networks and strategic alliances.* San Francisco: Jossey Bass.

Lipman, M. (1991). *Thinking in education.* New York: Cambridge University Press.

Madnick, S. E. (1991). The information platform. In M. S. S. Morton (Ed.), *The corporation of the 1990s: information technology and organizational transformation* (pp. 27–60). New York: Oxford University Press.

Mann, T. (1993). *Library research models: A guide to classification, cataloging, and computers.* New York: Oxford University Press.

Markey, K. (1986). Users and the online catalog: Subject access problems. In J. R. Mathews (Ed.), *The impact of online catalogs* (pp. 35–69). New York: Neal-Schuman.

Martel, L. (1986). *Mastering change.* New York: Mentor.

Martin, C. (1999). *Net future: The 7 cybertrends that will drive your business, create new wealth, and define your future.* New York: McGraw-Hill.

Martin, J. (1995). *The great transition: Using the seven disciplines of enterprise engineering to align people, technology, and strategy.* New York: Amacom.

Mayer, R. E. (1992). *Thinking, problem solving, cognition* (2nd ed.). New York: W. H. Freeman.

McFarlan, F. W. (1984). Information technology changes the way you compete. *Harvard Business Review, 62*, 98–103.

McGill, A. (1986, September–October). Some thoughts on creative organizational change. *Stage by Stage*, 16–17.

McGill, M. E., & Slocum, J. W., Jr. (1993). Unlearning the organization. *Organizational Dynamics, 22*, 67–79.

McGill, M. E., & Slocum, J. W., Jr. (1994). *The smarter organization: How to build a business that learns and adapts to marketplace needs.* New York: John Wiley & Sons.

McKenna, R. (1997). *Real time: Preparing for the age of the never satisfied customer.* Boston: Harvard Business School Press.

McKenzie, A. T. (1993). The academic on line. In G. P. Landow & P. Delany (Eds.), *The digital word: Text-based computing in the humanities* (pp. 201–216). Cambridge, MA: MIT Press.

McKinley, T. (1997). *From paper to Web: How to make information instantly accessible.* San Jose, CA: Adobe Press.

Miller, G. A. (1956, March). The magical number seven, plus or minus two: Some limits on our capacity for processing information. *Psychological Review, 63,* 81–97.

Miller, R. E. (1986). The tradition of reference service in the liberal arts college library. *RQ, 25* 387–401.

Mintzberg, H., Ahlstrand, B., & Lampel, J. (1998). *Strategy safari: A guided tour through the wilds of strategic management.* New York: Free Press.

Mitroff, I. I., & Linstone, H. A. (1993). *The unbounded mind: Breaking the chains of traditional business thinking.* New York: Oxford University Press.

Mooers, C. N. (1960). Mooer's law or why some retrieval systems are used and other are not. *American Documentation, 11,* ii.

Morris, D., & Brandon, J. (1993). *Re-engineering your business.* New York: McGraw-Hill.

Morton, M. S. S. (Ed.). (1991). *The corporation of the 1990s: Information technology and organizational transformation.* Oxford, England: Oxford University Press.

Moschella, D. C. (1997). *Waves of power: Dynamics of global technology leadership 1964–2010.* New York: Amacom.

Mougayar, W. (1997). *Opening digital markets: Battle plans and business strategies for Internet commerce.* (2nd ed.). New York: McGraw-Hill.

Nadler, D., & Tushman, M. (1990). Beyond the charismatic leader: Leadership and organizational change. *California Management Review, 31,* 77–97.

Nanus, B. (1992). *Visionary leadership: Creating a compelling sense of direction for your organization.* San Francisco: Jossey-Bass.

National Enquiry into Scholarly Communication. (1979). *Scholarly communication: The report of the national enquiry.* Baltimore: Johns Hopkins University Press.

Negroponte, N. (1995). *Being digital.* New York: Knopf.

Newell, A., & Simon, H. A. (1972). *Human problem solving.* Englewood Cliffs, NJ: Prentice-Hall.

Nielsen, J. (1995). *Multimedia and hypertext: The Internet and beyond.* Cambridge, MA: AP Professional.

Norman, D. A. (1993). *Things that make us smart: Defending human attributes in the age of the machine.* Reading, MA: Addison-Wesley.

Norman, D. A. (1998). *The invisible computer: Why good products can fail, the personal computer is so complex, and information appliances are the solution.* Cambridge, MA: MIT Press.

NRENAISSANCE Committee. (1994). *Realizing the information future: The Internet and beyond.* Washington, DC: National Academy Press.

Nwana, H. S. (1996). Software agents: An overview. *Knowledge Engineering Review, 3,* 205–244.

OCLC Newsletter. (1992, July–August). *Online Journal of Clinical Trials, 33.*

O'Dell, C. C., Grayson, J., Jr., & Essaides, N. (1998). *If only we knew what we know: The transfer of internal knowledge and best practice.* New York: Free Press.

Oliver, R. W. (1999). *The shape of things to come.* New York: McGraw-Hill.

Ohlson, K. (1998). Study sees bandwidth crunch in '99. 10 December, [http://cnn.com/TECH/computing/9812/10/bandwidth.idg/index.html].

Paisley, W. J. (1968). Information Needs and Uses. *Annual Review of Information Science and Technology, 3,* 1–30.

Papows, J. (1998). *Enterprise.com: Market leadership in the information age.* Reading, MA: Perseus Books.

Parsaye, K., & Chignell, M. (1993). *Intelligent database tools and applications.* New York: Wiley.

Parsaye, K. et al. (1989). *Intelligent databases: Object-oriented, deductive, hypermedia technologies.* New York: Wiley.

Pastine, M. (1987). Bibliographic instruction in the humanities. In C. A. Mellon (Ed.), *Bibliographic instruction: The second generation* (pp. 169–179). Littleton, CO: Libraries Unlimited.

Penniman, W. D. (1992). Shaping: The council on library resources helps to fund change. *Library Journal, 117,* 40–44.

Poetry software: for better or verse. (1994, September 27). *PC Magazine, 13,* 423.

Peppers, D., & Rogers, M. (1993). *The one to one future: Building relationships one customer at a time.* New York: Doubleday.

Peppers, D., & Rogers, M. (1997). *Enterprise one to one: Tools for competing in the interactive age.* New York: Doubleday.

Peters, T. (1987). *Thriving on chaos: Handbook for a management revolution.* New York: Alfred A. Knopf.

Peters, T. (1992). *Liberation management: Necessary disorganization for the nanosecond nineties.* New York: Alfred A. Knopf.

Peters, T. A. (1991). *The online catalog: A critical examination of public use.* Jefferson, NC: McFarland.

Petroski, H. (1990). *The pencil: A history of design and circumstance.* New York: Alfred A. Knopf.

Pinchot, G., & Pinchot, E. (1993). *The end of bureaucracy and the rise of the intelligent organization.* San Francisco: Berrett-Koehler.

Pinker, S. (1997). *How the mind works.* New York: W. W. Norton.

Porter, M. E., & Millar, V. E. (1985). How information gives you a competitive advantage. *Harvard Business Review, 63,* 149–160.

Pugh, E. W. (1995). *Building IBM: Shaping an industry and its technology.* Cambridge, MA: MIT Press.

Quinn, J. B. (1992). *Intelligent enterprises: A knowledge and service based paradigm for industry.* New York: Free Press.

Quinn, J. B., Jordan, J. B., & Zien, K. A. (1997). *Innovation explosion: Using intellect and software to revolutionize growth strategies.* New York: Free Press.

Reich, R. B. (1991). *The work of nations: Preparing ourselves for 21st century capitalism.* New York: Knopf.

Reichgelt, H. (1991). *Knowledge representation: An AI perspective.* Norwood, NJ: Ablex.

Robbins, J. (1994). Talk about the vision: The heart of your library. In D. Zweizig et al. (Eds.), *Tell it! Evaluation sourcebook and training manual* (pp. 13–25). Madison, WI: School of Library and Information Studies.

Robertson, D. S. (1998). *The new Renaissance: Computers and the next level of civilization.* New York: Oxford University Press.

Rogers, E. M. (1983). *Diffusion of innovations.* (3rd ed.). New York: Free Press.

Rosenberg, M. (1997, January 24). A classic, from A to Z: Britannica reborn in computers. *Miami Herald*, pp. 1F, 3F.

Rosenfeld, L., & Morville, P. (1998). *Information architecture for the World Wide Web.* Sebastopol, CA: O'Reilly & Associates.

Rubinstein, M. F. (1986). *Tools for thinking and problem solving.* Englewood Cliffs, NJ: Prentice-Hall.

Rudd, J., & Rudd, M. J. (1986). Coping with information load: User strategies and implications for librarians. *College and Research Libraries, 47*, 315–322.

Russo, J. E., & Schoemaker, P. J. H. (1989). *Decision traps: Ten barriers to brilliant decision-making and how to overcome them.* New York: Doubleday.

Salsin, J., & Cedar, T. (1985). Person-to-person communication in an applied-research service delivery setting. *Journal of the American Society for Information Science, 36*, 103–115.

Salton, G., & McGill, M. (1983). *Modern information retrieval.* New York: McGraw-Hill.

Savage, C. M. (1990). *Fifth generation management: Integrating enterprises through human networking.* Boston: Digital Press.

Schank, R. C., & Cleary, C. (1995). *Engines for education.* Hillsdale, NJ: Lawrence Erlbaum Associates.

Schenk, D. (1997). *Data smog: Surviving the information glut.* New York: HarperCollins.

Schön, D. (1971). *Beyond the stable state.* New York: Basic Books.

Seiler, L., & Surprenant, T. (1991). When we get the libraries we want, will we want the libraries we get? *Wilson Library Bulletin, 65*, 29–31, 152, 157.

Senge, P. M. (1990). *The fifth discipline: The art and practice of the learning organization.* New York: Doubleday Currency.

Senge, P. M. et al. (1994). *The fifth discipline fieldbook: Strategies and tools for building a learning organization.* New York: Doubleday.

Shapiro, C., & Varian, H. R. (1999). *Information rules: A strategic guide to the network economy.* Boston: Harvard Business School Press.

Silberman, S. (1999, January 7). Turning over a new leaf. In *Wired News.* [Online] Available: http://www.wired.com/news/culture/story/15501.html.

Simon, H. A. (1997). *Administrative behavior: A study of decision-making processes in administrative organizations.* (4th ed.). New York: Free Press.

Sims, H. P., & Lorenzi, P. (1992). *The new leadership paradigm: Social learning and cognition in organizations.* Newbury Park, CA: Sage.

Slack, J. (1984). *Communication technologies and society: Conceptions of causality and the politics of technological intervention.* Norwood, NJ: Ablex.

Smith, M. R., & Marx, L. (Eds.) (1994). *Does technology drive history? The dilemma of technological determinism.* Cambridge, MA: MIT Press.

Sosa, J., & Harris, M. H. (1991). Jose Ortega y Gasset and the role of the librarian in post-industrial America. *Libri, 41*, 3–21.

Spitzer, Q., & Evans, R. (1997). *Heads, you win!: How the best companies think.* New York: Simon & Schuster.

Sterne, J. (1999). *World Wide Web marketing.* (2nd ed.). New York: Wiley.

Stewart, T. A. (1997). *Intellectual capital: The new wealth of organizations.* New York: Doubleday.

Stoffle, C. J., Renaud, R, & Veldof, J. R. (1996). Choosing our futures. *College and Research Libraries, 57,* 213–25.

Talbott, S. L. (1995). *The future does not compute: Transcending the machines in our midst.* Sebastopol, CA: O'Reilly & Associates.

Tapscott, D. (1996). *The digital economy: Promise and peril in the age of networked intelligence.* New York: McGraw-Hill.

Tapscott, D., & Caston, A. (1993). *Paradigm shift: The new promise of information technology.* New York: McGraw-Hill.

The technology payoff: A sweeping reorganization of work itself is boosting productivity. (1993, June 14). *Business Week, No. 3323,* 56–79.

Te'eni, D., & Speltz, N. F. (1993). Management information systems in cultural institutions. In D. R. Young, R. M. Hollister, & V. A. Hodgkinson (Eds.), *Governing, leading, and managing nonprofit organizations* (pp. 77–92). San Francisco: Jossey-Bass Publishers.

Theim, J. (1979). The great library of Alexandria burnt: Towards the history of a symbol. *Journal of the History of Ideas, 40,* 507–526.

Tomer, C. (1993). Emerging electronic library services and the idea of location independence. In G. P. Landow & P. Delany (Eds.), *The digital word: Text-based computing in the humanities* (pp. 139–161). Cambridge, MA: MIT Press.

Tweney, D. (1999, 1 January). A look (back) at Net business: Mergers, departures, trials—we ain't seen nothin' yet. CNN Interactive [Online]. Available: http://cnn.com/TECH/computing/9901/01/netbiz.idg/index.html.

Ulrich, D., von Glinow, M. A., & Jick, T. (1993). High-impact learning: Building and diffusing learning capability. *Organizational Dynamics, 22,* 52–66.

Van Arsdale, W. O., & Ostrye, A. T. (1986). InfoTrac: A second opinion. *American Libraries, 17,* 514–515.

Van der Heijden, K. (1996.). *Scenarios: The art of strategic conversation.* New York: Wiley.

Van Rijsbergen, C. J. (1979). *Information retrieval.* (2nd ed.). London: Butterworths.

Vaskevitch, D. (1993). *Client/server strategies.* San Mateo, CA: IDG Books Worldwide.

Ventura, C. A. (1988). Why switch from paper to electronic manuals? *Proceedings ACM Conference Document Processing Systems.* Santa Fe, NM, 5–9 December, 111–116.

Walton, R. E. (1989). *Up and running: Integrating information technology and the organization.* Boston: Harvard Business School Press.

Watkins, K. E., & Marsick, V. J. (1993). *Sculpting the learning organization: Lessons in the art and science of systemic change.* San Francisco: Jossey-Bass.

Watson-Boone, R. (1994). The information needs and habits of humanities scholars. *RQ, 34,* 213.

Weaver, J. (1998, 28 December). Web marketing holdouts shift sights. [www.msnbc.com/news/225981.asp].

Weeks, L. (1991, May 26). Endangered species? The Library of Congress and the future of the book. *Washington Post Magazine,* 10–31.

Weinberg, G. M., & Weinberg, D. (1979). *On the design of stable systems.* New York: Wiley.

Weisbord, M. R. (1987). *Productive workplaces: Organizing and managing for dignity, meaning, and community.* San Francisco: Jossey-Bass.

Whiteley, R. C. (1991). *The customer-driven company: Moving from talk to action.* Reading, MA: Addison-Wesley.

Wilberly, S. E., & Dougherty, R. A. (1988). Users' persistence in scanning lists of references. *College and Research Libraries, 49,* 149–156.

Wilson, E. O. (1998). *Consilience: The unity of knowledge.* New York: Knopf.

Winner, L. (1986). *The whale and the reactor: The search for limits in an age of high technology.* Cambridge, MA: MIT Press.

Winograd, T., & Flores, F. (1986). *Understanding computers and cognition: A new foundation for design.* Reading, MA: Addison-Wesley.

Woodsworth, A. et al. (1989). The model research library: Planning for the future. *Journal of Academic Librarianship, 15,* 132–138.

Wren, D. A. (1979). *The evolution of management thought.* (2nd ed.). New York: Wiley.

Yankelovich, N. (1994). From electronic books to electronic library: Revisiting 'reading and writing the electronic book.' In P. Delany & G. P. Landow (Eds.), *Hypermedia and literary studies* (pp. 133–118). Cambridge, MA: MIT Press.

Zimmermann, M. (1993). The freetext personal information retrieval. In G. P. Landow & P. Delany, *The digital word: Text-based computing in the humanities* (pp. 53–68). Cambridge, MA: MIT Press.

Author Index

165

Subject Index